An OPUS book

Introduction to English Law

Sir David Yardley was formerly Chairman of the
Commission for Local Administration in England. He is a
barrister of Gray's Inn, and author of *Introduction to
Constitutional and Administrative Law* (1995).

Introduction to
English Law

(Originally *Elements of English Law*)

ELEVENTH EDITION PREPARED BY
SIR DAVID YARDLEY

William Geldart

Oxford   New York
OXFORD UNIVERSITY PRESS
1995

Oxford University Press, Walton Street, Oxford OX2 6DP

Oxford New York
Athens Auckland Bangkok Bombay
Calcutta Cape Town Dar es Salaam Delhi
Florence Hong Kong Istanbul Karachi
Kuala Lumpur Madras Madrid Melbourne
Mexico City Nairobi Paris Singapore
Taipei Tokyo Toronto
and associated companies in
Berlin Ibadan

Oxford is a trade mark of Oxford University Press

© Oxford University Press 1966, 1991, 1995

First edition published 1911
Seventh edition issued as an Oxford University Press paperback 1966
Eighth edition 1975
Ninth edition (under the title Introduction to English Law) 1984
Tenth edition 1991
Eleventh edition 1995

British Library Cataloguing in Publication Data
Data available

Library of Congress Cataloging in Publication Data
Geldart, William, 1870–1922
Introduction to English law : (originally Elements of English law)/
William Geldart.— 11th ed. / prepared by Sir David Yardley.
p. cm.
"An OPUS book" —P. [1]
Includes bibliographical references.
1. Law—Great Britain. I. Yardley, D. C. M. (David Charles Miller) II. Title.
KD661.G4 1995 95–10503
349.42—dc20[344.2]
ISBN 0–19–289268–1

Typeset by Pure Tech India Ltd, Pondicherry
Printed in Great Britain by
Biddles Ltd.,
Guildford and King's Lynn

Preface to eleventh edition

When after William Geldart's death Sir William Holdsworth was called upon to prepare a second edition of this little book, he wrote in the Preface that it was a striking testimony to the extent of Geldart's knowledge of the English legal system, and to his powers of clear, well-proportioned, and accurate exposition; and Professor H. G. Hanbury, a later editor of the book, considered that Geldart was the master of legal analysis. Certainly the success of the book on its appearance in 1911 can to some extent be judged by the necessity to reprint it no less than eleven times before Holdsworth prepared the second edition. This was published in 1929, and Holdsworth's greatest contribution to the text was his transformation of Chapter 5 from an account of the old property law to that of the new era ushered in by the 1925 Property Acts. Holdsworth produced a third edition just before the Second World War, and thereafter Hanbury prepared three more. For the last thirty years it has been my privilege to take the book over and to do the work on it necessary for five more editions.

This eleventh edition is in many respects much changed from the book as it first appeared, and yet I hope its original essence remains. It is still my aim that it should expound the elements of the main areas of English law readably, accurately, and yet in short form. The overall length of the book has increased only a little since 1911, and there are parts of Chapter 2 and 3 which have been altered only marginally since Geldart wrote them. But the substance of the rest of the book is for the most part quite different from that first presented. Even the book's title has been altered, as has the title of Chapter 3.

Legislation needing to be incorporated since the last edition includes the Computer Misuse Act 1990; the Courts and Legal

Services Act 1990, introducing the Legal Services Ombudsman; the Criminal Justice Act 1991; the Football (Offences) Act 1991; the Road Traffic Act 1991; the Dangerous Dogs Act 1991; the Child Support Act 1991, creating the controversial Child Support Agency; the Cheques Act 1992; the Access to Neighbouring Land Act 1992; the Charities Acts 1992 and 1993; the Leasehold Reform, Housing, and Urban Development Act 1993; the European Communities (Amendment) Act 1993, which provides for the legal consequences of the Maastricht Treaty; the Law Reform (Miscellaneous Provisions) Act 1994; the Trade Marks Act 1994; the Criminal Justice and Public Order Act 1994; the Sale of Goods (Amendment) Act 1994; and the Marriage Act 1994, substantially relaxing former restrictions upon the kinds of places where marriage may take place. Case law has also developed significantly, and there have been important decisions on the liability for negligence causing nervous shock, and the effect of mistake upon a contract. The rules of statutory interpretation have been revised and restated, and the circumstances in which death may be found to have resulted from involuntary manslaughter have been narrowed.

A striking feature of developments in the past few years has been the wealth of reform on divers areas of law recommended by the Law Commission. On a few occasions such recommendations have resulted in reasonably prompt implementation by Parliament, but unfortunately there have been far too many reports which have not been followed by the necessary legislation even though they have for the most part been greeted with near-universal approval on publication. It is understandable that successive Governments and Parliaments have been preoccupied with other business and with perhaps more politically motivated legislation, but the Law Commissions Act 1965 was always intended to facilitate properly considered law reform. Adequate provision to ensure that Law Commission reports, which usually include draft Bills, are sent on their way towards enactment with some dispatch is long overdue. At the time of writing the Government has recently introduced five short Bills into Parliament in order to enact some of the recommendations of the Law

Commission which have been outstanding, and it is to be hoped that they reach the statute book, but there still remain many other measures which need to be tackled.

As it is, this edition refers to quite a number of reforms of the law which are pending but not yet achieved. The march of legal development and law reform has been so rapid during this latter part of the twentieth century that it easily rivals the pace and sweeping character of that earlier notable period of law reform in the late nineteenth century, but it could have been even more rapid and far-reaching.

Oxford   D.C.M.Y.
April 1995

Contents

1 Statute law and common law

1. *Law and laws*

We commonly speak of both law and laws—the English Law, or the Laws of England; and these terms, though not used with precision, point to two different aspects under which legal science may be approached. The laws of a country are thought of as separate, distinct, individual rules; the law of a country, however much we may analyse it into separate rules, is something more than the mere sum of such rules. It is rather a whole, a system which orders our conduct; in which the separate rules have their place and their relation to each other and to the whole; which is never completely exhausted by any analysis, however far the analysis may be pushed, and however much the analysis may be necessary to our understanding of the whole. Thus each rule which we call *a* law is a part of the whole we call *the* law. Lawyers generally speak of *law*; laymen more often of *laws*.

There is also a more precise way in which we use this distinction between law and laws. Some laws are presented to us as having from the beginning a separate and independent existence; they are not derived by any process of analysis or development from the law as a whole. We know when they were made and by whom, though when made they have to take their place in the legal system; they become parts of *the* law. Such laws in this country are for the most part what we call Acts of Parliament, or, as they are called generally by lawyers, statutes; collectively they are spoken of as Statute Law. On the other hand, putting aside for the present the rules of Equity, the great body of law which is not Statute Law is called the Common Law. The Common Law has grown rather than been made. We cannot point to any definite time when it began; as far back as our reports go we find judges assuming that there is a Common Law not made by any legislator. When we speak of an individual law we generally mean a statute; when we speak of *the* law we are thinking of the system of law which includes both Statute and Common Law, though the bulk of the former is rapidly overtaking that of the latter. A rule of the Common Law would rarely, if ever, be spoken of as *a* law.

This distinction between law as a system and law as enactments is brought out more clearly in those languages which use different words for each: the French *droit*, the German *Recht*, mean 'law': *loi* and *Gesetz* mean 'a law'.

2. *The relations between statute law and common law*

(1) In spite of the enormous and ever-growing bulk of the Statute Law—our statutes begin with the reissue of Magna Carta in 1225 in the reign of Henry III, and a large volume is now added every year—much of the fundamental part of our law is still Common Law. No statute, for instance, yet prescribes in general terms that a man must pay his debts or perform his contracts or pay damages for trespass or libel or slander. The statutes assume the existence of the Common Law. Except in so far as they restate in the form of a code some particular branch of the law, they are the addenda and errata of the book of the Common Law; and they would have no meaning except by reference to the Common Law. If all the statutes of the realm were repealed, we should still have a system of law, though, it may be, an unworkable one; if we could imagine the Common Law swept away and the Statute Law preserved, we should have only disjointed rules torn from their context, and no provision at all for many of the most important relations of life. The Law Commissions Act 1965, however, established a body of Commissioners whose task it is to prepare legislation which shall reform and simplify the law,

and the Commissioners stated, in announcing their first pro-
gramme of work, that they intended to prepare a codification of
the laws of contract and of landlord and tenant. These major
codes have not yet been completed (the Annual Report of the
Law Commission for 1972–3 stated that work on the preparation
of a code of the law of contract had been suspended, and so it
is now doubtful whether it will ever be completed), but certain
codes dealing with more restricted areas of law have been
enacted in recent years, e.g. the Theft Act 1968, the Animals Act
1971, the Forgery and Counterfeiting Act 1981, and the Criminal
Attempts Act 1981; and the Law Commission has more recently
expressed the intention to work towards a complete code of
criminal law. The work of the Law Commission has in recent
years also led to much obsolete legislation being repealed. For
example, much of the old Sunday Observance legislation was
swept away by the Statute Law (Repeals) Act 1969.

(2) Where Statute Law and Common Law come into competition, it is the former that prevails. Our law sets no limits to the
power of Parliament. As the constitutionalist A. V. Dicey wrote
a century ago, 'The sovereignty of Parliament is (from a legal
point of view) the dominant characteristic of our political institutions.' No court or judge can refuse to enforce an Act of
Parliament, though in the exercise of its duty to interpret an Act
a court may sometimes alter considerably the effect that the
legislators had intended the Act to have. No development of the
Common Law can repeal an Act of Parliament, but large parts of
the Common Law have from time to time been abolished by Act
of Parliament, and their place has been taken by statutory rules.

This supremacy of the statute-making power is not a logical or
even a practical necessity. It is well known that under the
Constitution of the United States neither Congress nor the State
Legislatures have an unlimited power of legislation. The unlimited legislative power of Parliament is a rule of our Constitutional Law. It is quite conceivable, and it was at one time
supposed to be the case, that there were principles of the
Common Law which would control an Act of Parliament, but in

fact judges have, from an early period, recognized and acquiesced in the sovereignty of Parliament.

There are of course obvious practical limitations upon the power of Parliament, and in particular it is doubtless highly desirable since the United Kingdom's entry to the European Communities in 1973 that parliamentary legislation should accord with the needs, not only of this country, but also of our European partners. The courts will also not infrequently interpret statutes in such a way as to be in line with modern needs, which may differ from those in existence when the Acts were passed. The European Communities have in 1994 been restyled as the European Union, and recent decisions both of the European Court of Justice and the English courts have asserted that the courts have a duty to apply European Union law in preference to any inconsistent domestic legislation. To this extent only, therefore, a court may refuse to apply the provisions of a statute. In every other case it is in fact and in law absolutely bound by any Act which has not been repealed by Parliament itself. Furthermore, the ultimate legislature sovereignty of Parliament must remain because it would always be open to Parliament to amend or repeal the legislation by which the United Kingdom joined the European Union.

(3) How do we know the law? Here there is a great difference between Statute and Common Law. A statute is drawn up in a definite form of words, and these words have been approved by Parliament and have received the Royal assent. In general there is no difficulty in ascertaining the words of a statute. At the present day two identical printed copies are made, each bearing a certificate of the Clerk of Parliaments that the Royal assent has been given, and in the last resort reference can be made to these copies for the purpose of ascertaining the true words of the statutes. For practical purposes any copy made by the Queen's printer is sufficient. In the case of some old statutes there is a possible doubt not only as to the exact words of a statute, but even whether such a statute was ever made; but in practice such doubts hardly ever arise.

Still the words of the statute are not the statute itself; the law expressed by the words is not the same thing as the words which express it. Thus a person imperfectly acquainted with English may know the words of the statute, but he will not know the law. The same is true to a greater or less degree of anyone who comes to the reading of a statute without sufficient legal knowledge. The interpretation of a statute requires not only a knowledge of the meaning of legal technical terms, but also of the whole system of law of which the statute forms a part; in particular it requires a knowledge of the legal rules of interpretation, which are themselves rules of law. Some of these are Common Law rules; some are themselves statutory. Thus there was a Common Law rule that in interpreting a statute no account must be taken of anything said in debate while the statute was passing through its various stages in Parliament; as far as possible the words of the statute had to speak for themselves. Fortunately the courts themselves amended this rule in 1992, and now they may consult the verbatim record of debates in Parliament in order to construe Acts appearing to be ambiguous or obscure, or to lead to absurdity. So there is a statutory rule that in Acts made since 1850, unless a contrary intention appears, masculine words shall include the feminine, words in the singular shall include the plural, words in the plural shall include the singular.

Even lawyers may differ as to the meaning of a statute. If such a question arises for the first time in a lawsuit, the judge will have to decide the meaning in accordance with the recognized rules of interpretation, and his decision will be a binding authority for all future cases in which the same question arises, just as we shall see that a judge's decision is a binding authority for future cases where a question arises as to the Common Law. In this way many statutes—especially the older ones—have become overlaid with a mass of judicial interpretation which cannot be departed from.

On the other hand we have no authoritative text of the Common Law. There is no one form of words in which it has as a whole been expressed at any time. Therefore in a sense one may speak of the Common Law as unwritten law in contrast with Statute Law, which is written law. Nevertheless the sources from which we derive our knowledge of the Common Law are in writing or print. First among these come the reported decisions of the judges of the English courts. Ever since the reign of Edward I there have been lawyers who have made it their business to report the discussions in court and the judgments given in cases which seemed of legal interest. The earliest of these reports are the Year-Books. They are reports of cases made by anonymous reporters from the time of Edward I to that of Henry VIII. These are followed by reports produced by lawyers reporting under their own names. They were at first published (like textbooks) only as and when the author, or the representatives of a deceased author, saw fit to do so. It was not until the end of the eighteenth century that reports began to be regularly published contemporaneously with the decisions of the cases reported. At the beginning these reports seem to have served mainly the purpose of instruction and information. The fact that a judge had stated that such and such was the law was evidence, but not more than evidence, that such was the law. He might have been mistaken; another judge might perhaps decide differently. But in course of time we find a change in the attitude of judges and lawyers towards reported decisions. The citation of decided cases becomes more frequent; greater and greater weight is attached to them as authorities. From the sixteenth century onwards we may say that decided cases are regarded as a definite authority, which, at least in the absence of special reasons to the contrary, must be followed for the future. For the last 350 years, at any rate, the decisions of judges of the higher courts have had a binding force for all similar cases which may arise in the future.

3. *The binding force of precedents*

This binding force is not, however, in all cases an irresistible one. The decisions of the highest appellate court in the country for the overwhelming majority of English cases—the House of

Lords—are absolutely binding on all lower courts, and usually upon itself. (The House of Lords, like all other municipal courts, is subordinate on matters of European law to the Court of Justice of the European Communities.) But in 1966 the House decided that it would in future consider itself able to depart from any previous decision of the House when it appeared right to do so. There have been several notable instances when it has exercised this new-found power, and the general result has been a relaxation of the former strict binding nature of precedent, as well as of the rules of statutory interpretation mentioned above. So, too, the decisions of the Court of Appeal, which stands, for civil cases and for some criminal cases, next below the House of Lords, are binding declarations of the law for all lower courts, and even for itself. There are, however, certain circumstances in which a decision of the Court of Appeal, e.g. when given in conflict with what it had previously decided, has not been followed, even by a lower court; and in 1992 the Court of Appeal itself decided it would not be bound to follow one of its previous decisions in a case involving someone's liberty if injustice might thereby result.

Decisions rendered by Divisional Courts, which consist of two or three judges of the High Court sitting usually to review the proceeding of an inferior tribunal or to hear an appeal from the decision of magistrates in a summary criminal trial, usually follow those made in earlier Divisional Court cases, but in 1984 it was held that a Divisional Court is not strictly bound by such earlier decisions. A decision of one High Court judge, though treated by another as of high persuasive authority, is again not absolutely binding on him.

A decision of a lower court is not, in the first instance, binding on any court ranking above it. But in the course of time it may acquire an authority which even a higher court will not disregard. It may happen that a question has never been carried up to the Court of Appeal or to the House of Lords, but that the lower courts have repeatedly decided it in the same way; or it may be that even a single decision of a lower court has remained for a long time unquestioned. In such a case the necessary result will be that lawyers and the public have come to regard such a decision as law, and have acted as if it was law. People will have made contracts, carried on business, disposed of their property, on the faith of such a decision, and the reversal of the rule would involve enormous hardship. It is sometimes more important that the law should be certain than that it should be perfect. The consequence is that even a higher court, though it may think a decision of a lower court wrong in principle, may refuse to overrule it, holding that the evil of upsetting what everyone has treated as established is greater than the evil of allowing a mistaken rule to stand. The best cure in such a case is an alteration of the law by statute, for an alteration by statute does not work the same hardship as a reversal by a higher court of what was supposed to be the law. A statute need not, and as a rule does not, affect anything done before it was passed. Previous transactions remain governed by the law in force at the time they were made. But the theory or fiction of our case law is that the judge does not make new laws, but only declares what was already law; so that if a higher court overrules the decision of a lower court, it declares that what was supposed to be law never really was law, and consequently past transactions will be governed by a rule contrary to what the parties believed to be law.

4. *Ratio decidendi* and *obiter dictum*

If you open a volume of the Law Reports and read the report of a case, how will you discover the law which the decision lays down? How will you find what is called the *ratio decidendi*—the principle on which the decision is based? Remember that the judge is not a legislator. It is not his business—in form at any rate—to *make* rules of law; his first duty is to decide the dispute between the parties. The dispute may be largely a question of fact. In some cases the questions of fact will have been already answered by a jury; in others the judge himself will have to decide questions of fact. At any rate the judgment will involve the application of principles of law to concrete facts. The reader of a Law Report must therefore first disentangle the law stated in a judgment from the facts to which it is applied. That may be a difficult matter. No form is prescribed in which judgements must be delivered, and it may often be a matter of doubt how far a decision turns on the view which the judge took of the facts, and how far on a rule of law which he considered applicable. The headnote which is put at the beginning of a report of a case generally contains a statement of the rule supposed to be involved. But this headnote is not part of the report; it is merely the reporter's own view of the effect of the judgment. In using a Law Report, therefore, everyone is free, where there is room for doubt, to hold his own view of what was the law laid down in any particular case, unless and until the doubt has been settled by a subsequent decision.

From the *ratio decidendi* we must carefully distinguish what are called *dicta* or *obiter dicta*—'things said by the way'.

An *obiter dictum*, strictly speaking, is a statement of the law made in the course of a judgment, not professing to be applicable to the actual question between the parties, but made by way of explanation or illustration or general exposition of the law. Such *dicta* have no binding force, though they have an authority which is entitled to respect and which will vary according to the reputation of the particular judge.

We sometimes find that a judge in deciding a case will profess to decide it on a principle really wider than is necessary for the purpose, when it might have been decided on some already recognized but much narrower ground. In such a case the supposed principle is in effect equivalent to an *obiter dictum*; it will not be treated as the true *ratio decidendi* of the case.

But a reason given by a single judge for his decision is not to be regarded as *obiter* merely because he has given an additional reason in the same judgment. Where there are several judges, and they agree in the result, but give different reasons, the matter is left open for a judge in a subsequent case to decide which reason is the right one.

5. *How far do the judges make the law?*

I have spoken hitherto of judicial decisions, not only as the source from which we get our knowledge of the Common Law, but also as binding authorities. But this is consistent with two different views of the relation of the judges to the law. First, and this is the older theory, we may suppose that a judicial decision is no more than a declaration and evidence—but conclusive evidence—of what already exists; the Common Law as a whole, it is said, has existed from time immemorial in the minds of judges and lawyers—perhaps in the minds of the people at large so far as they could understand it—and every decision is merely a manifestation of it. We find this view in Hale's *History of the Common Law* (1713) and in Blackstone's *Commentaries* (1765). Secondly, we find Bentham and Austin speaking of

the childish fiction employed by our judges that Judiciary or Common Law is not made by them, but is a miraculous something made by nobody, existing I suppose from eternity and merely declared from time to time by the judges.

According to the view of these writers and others who have followed them, for instance Salmond and Gray, judges are really law-makers, and in laying down the law exercise a function almost, if not exactly, like that of the legislator in making new law from time to time. The two points of view were admirably stated in Maine's *Ancient Law* (1908):

With respect to that great portion of our legal system which is enshrined in cases and recorded in Law Reports, we habitually employ a double language, and entertain, as it would appear, a double and inconsistent set of ideas. When a group of facts come before our English court for adjudication, the whole course of the discussion between the judge and the advocates assumes that no question is, or can be raised which will call for the application of any principles but old ones, or of any distinctions but such as have long since been allowed. It is taken absolutely for granted that there is somewhere a rule of known law which will cover the facts of the dispute now litigated, and that, if such a rule be not discovered, it is only that the necessary patience, knowledge, or acumen is not forthcoming to detect it. Yet the moment the judgement has been rendered and reported, we slide unconsciously or unavowedly into a new language and a new train of thought. We now admit that the new decision has modified the law. The rules applicable have—to use the very inaccurate expression sometimes employed—become more elastic; in fact, they have been changed. A clear addition has been made to the precedents, and the canon or law elicited by comparing the precedents is not the same with that which would have been obtained if the series of cases had been curtailed by a single example.

Neither of these views is the whole truth. On the one hand it is, of course, untrue that our Common Law has always been the same, even if we disregard the changes made by statute. No one can seriously imagine that the Common Law of 600 years ago would have had an intelligible answer to many of the legal questions of modern life. We know as a matter of fact that it answered some questions in the opposite sense to that in which we now answer them, e.g. a simple executory contract had no legal effect then, and we can trace the steps by which it acquired legal effect. On the other hand, to say that a judge in deciding is ever doing anything analogous to legislation is really doing violence to the facts. In the majority of cases where a new precedent is established, the process is obviously that of applying existing acknowledged principles to a new set of facts. The principles, it may be, give no explicit answer to the question put. It does not follow that they give no answer at all. By a process of deduction, by argument from analogy, the existing principles may be made to yield a new principle, which is new because never explicitly stated before, but which in another sense is not new because it was already involved in what was already acknowledged. Just in the same way the conclusions of a science may be involved in its premisses, and yet when first made constitute something new, an addition to what was before acknowledged. Even where a decision does not follow a definite logical process from acknowledged principles it has not the arbitrary character of legislation. In the absence of clear precedents which might govern a question, we find judges relying on such considerations as the opinions of legal writers, the practice of conveyancers, the law of other modern countries, the Roman Law, principles of 'natural justice' or public policy. The proper application of these may be a matter of dispute and difficulty but in any case the judge is applying a standard; he shows that he is not free to decide as he pleases, as a legislator would be; he is bound to decide according to principle. If we say that the judge really *makes* the law like a legislator, we shall be bound to say that the facts of the case were previously governed by no law; they fell outside the realm of law when they occurred, and are only brought within it when the decision is given. To argue that this is so, because before the decision no one knew with certainty what the law was, is like arguing that a piece of land is valueless until it has been sold, or until a valuer has made a valuation of it, because until then no one knows with certainty for what it will be sold or at what figure it will be valued. In truth the parties in fixing the price, or the valuer in making the valuation, have really tried to discover something already existing. The analogy goes further; just as the price or the valuation, even though mistaken, will be a new element which will help to determine the value for the future, so the judge's decision on the law on a given question, whether right or wrong, fixes or helps to fix the law for the future.

Again the view that until a rule is laid down in a legal decision there is no law governing the facts of the case will really lead to the conclusion that no concrete set of facts is governed by any law until a decision has been given, because in every case the process of decision involves the mental process of bringing the particular facts within some principle. Suppose, on the one hand, a question whether A's conduct amounted to an acceptance of an offer; on the other, whether a given transaction is contrary to public policy. There is an apparent, but not a real difference. In the former case the existing principles are so well defined that it looks as if the facts automatically, as it were, fall into the pigeon-hole which the law provides; in the latter the principle is so wide that in order to apply it the judge must explicitly and openly say, 'conduct which has such and such qualities is contrary to public policy', and so frame a rule which defines and develops the conception of public policy. But in the former case the same process has really been gone through. The act does not really fall automatically into the pigeon-hole; the judge must have had in his mind the qualities of an act which will make it an acceptance; the judge really says, 'conduct such as that in this case amounts to an acceptance'. The bringing of concrete facts under a rule is always a mental process, and a process of generalization. In this way every case which is decided means a development of the principle which is applied. The practical difference is that in the majority of cases the application is so easy, and the development of the existing principle is so infinitesimal, that the case is not worth reporting, and therefore, for *practical* purposes, adds nothing to the law.

A distinction is sometimes made between 'declaratory' precedents, which merely declare existing law, and 'original' precedents which lay down new law. In truth the difference is one of degree and not of kind. If we have a case which deals with certain facts by applying an acknowledged rule, we really have an addition to the rule, because we now know that a certain kind of fact falls within it, and in the nature of things we can never have two sets of facts which are precisely similar. No precedent is purely 'declaratory' or purely 'original'.

The contradiction between the view that judges merely declare the Common Law, and the view that they make new law in the same way as a legislator does, is solved by the conception of evolution of development which was not familiar either to the old lawyers, such as Blackstone, or to their critics, such as Bentham and Austin. The essence of that conception is that a thing may change and yet remain the same thing. To ask whether our law of today is the same law as the English law of 600 years ago is, to use a phrase of Sir Frederick Pollock, 'like discussing whether the John Milton who wrote *Samson Agonistes* was really the same John Milton who wrote *Lycidas*'. It is the same and not the same. Every legal decision is a step in the process of growth. In every case it is true that there is already a law applicable to the facts; it is equally true that, when the decision has been given, the law is not precisely what it was before. The '*double language*' which Maine refers to as evidence of a deep-seated fiction is really an expression of a fundamental truth.

6. *Advantages and disadvantages of case law*

The system of Case Law is peculiar to England and the countries which have derived their law from England. Its essential principle is the rule that decided cases are binding authorities for the future. In other countries this is not so, or was not so until recently. In other countries the judge, in his application and interpretation both of enacted law and of the general principles which will always underlie and supplement enacted law, is not bound by previous decisions of the same or any other court, but is free and indeed is bound to decide according to the best of his own judgement.

The great advantages of a system of Case Law in the English sense are four:

(1) *Certainty.* The fact that decided cases are binding or highly persuasive authorities for the future makes it certain or at least highly probable that every future case which is essentially similar will be decided in the same way. People may therefore regulate their conduct with confidence upon the law once laid down by the judges.

(2) *The possibility of growth.* Wherever the way is not closed by statute or precedent, new rules of law will from time to time be authoritatively laid down to meet new circumstances and the changing needs of society. Where there is no system of Case Law the work of the judge who decides a case leaves no lasting mark on the law for the future: it is, as far as the development of the law goes, thrown away.

(3) *A great wealth of detailed rules.* Our law is much richer in detail than any code of law (unless based on Case Law) can possibly be. The German Civil Code, for instance, consists of less than 2,500 paragraphs.

(4) *Their practical character*. Because the rules laid down by the cases are the product, not solely of academic speculation, but of difficulties which have actually arisen, they are practical rules which are in close touch with the needs of everyday life.

The great disadvantages of Case Law are:

(1) *Rigidity*. Where a rule has once been decided, even though wrongly, it is difficult to depart from it, though the difficulty has been eased by the courts in recent years, as we have seen. The binding force of a precedent is a fetter on the discretion of the judge; but for precedent he would have a much freer hand.

(2) *The danger of illogical distinctions*. When a rule which is binding is felt to work hardship, a judge will often avoid applying it to cases which logically ought to fall within it, by laying hold of minute distinctions which will enable him to say that the later case is different from the earlier case in which the rule was established. Every now and then a precedent leads one into a blind alley, from which one has to escape as best one can. So, too, rules which are logically inconsistent with each other are sometimes developed along distinct lines of cases, which ultimately meet and come into conflict.

(3) *Bulk and complexity*. The wealth of detail, and the fact that the rules of law are to be found scattered over more than 2,000 volumes of law reports, make the law extraordinarily cumbrous and difficult to learn and apply.

The advantages of our system far outweigh the disadvantages, yet the disadvantages are serious. The cure for them is to be found, and has from time to time been found, in Statute Law. Where rules have been definitely laid down which produce hardship, where the rules have been made complicated and illogical by attempts to avoid hardship, Statute Law must intervene to remove the hardship or to lay down simple and intelligible rules; and the Law Commission set up in 1965 has now greatly facilitated the attainment of these objects. Its predecessor was the Law Revision Committee, set up in 1933 (and revived after the Second World War as the Law Reform

Committee) to make proposals for the reform of branches of law which, for any of these reasons, needed reconsideration; and some of its proposals became statutes which have made salutary changes in the law (for instance, changes as to the status of married women, pp. 56–60, corporations' contracts, pp. 71–5, the survival of causes of action in tort, pp. 159–60, limitations of actions, pp. 160–1, contributory negligence, p. 156–7, enforcement of contracts, p. 135, liability of occupiers of premises, p. 156, misrepresentation, pp. 7–8, 139–40). So, again, where the law has been satisfactorily worked out in detail, but the mass of scattered decisions is unmanageable, Statute may undertake the work of codification, an orderly arrangement of the established rules in statutory form. In this way some considerable portions of the Common Law have from time to time been converted into Statute Law without material alteration of substance; the labour of searching for decisions is removed or lessened, and the law is to some extent made accessible to persons who are not professional lawyers. Examples of such codification may be found in the Bills of Exchange Act 1882, the Sale of Goods Act 1893 (now repealed and replaced by the Sale of Goods Act 1979, and added to by the Supply of Goods and Services Act 1982), and to some extent in the series of Property Acts which came into force in 1926. (For these Acts see below, p. 86 n. 1.) But these last-mentioned Acts are only partly codifying Acts. We shall see that they effect great and far-reaching changes in the Land Law. As has been mentioned above, further major codification can be expected in due course as a result of the work of the Law Commission. Already some parts of the criminal law have been codified as a result of its efforts.

How far the Common Law as a whole is capable of being or is likely to be codified in this way is a question which cannot be here discussed. But, at any rate, two conditions of a satisfactory codification may here be indicated:

(1) It must reproduce without material loss the richness of detail which is a characteristic merit of our system of Case Law; we should not be content with a code of the brief and abstract kind

which has been adopted and used with success in some foreign countries.

(2) The adoption of a code must not deprive us of the advantages which we at present enjoy from the principle of binding precedents: i.e. judicial decisions interpreting the code will still be binding, and will still be a means by which the law will develop, will still be capable of enriching the law by framing detailed rules.

7. *Other sources of the common law*

The decisions of courts of other countries which administer a law derived from or related to our own, such as the Scottish, Irish, Commonwealth, and American courts, though not binding upon our courts, are entitled to great respect. Even the judgments given by the Judicial Committee of the Privy Council, which acts as a final Court of Appeal from those parts of the Commonwealth whose highest courts have not final authority, are not binding upon our courts; but the fact that the members of that tribunal are, to a large extent, the same persons as the members of the House of Lords when it sits as an appeal court, greatly increases their authority. The House of Lords is a common court of final appeal in civil matters for England and Wales, Scotland, and Northern Ireland—and for England and Wales and Northern Ireland in criminal matters; where the principles involved are substantially the same, or where the question turns on a statute common to England and one or both of these other countries, the Lords' decision on a Scottish or Irish case will be treated as binding authority for English cases.

Some of the works of the older writers, such as the *Commentary* written by Coke in the seventeenth century on the fifteenth-century treatise of Littleton on *Tenures*, and Sir Michael Foster's work on *Crown Law* written in the eighteenth century, are known as 'books of authority', and have a force nearly equal in binding effect to judicial decisions. Other treatises on law have a merely 'persuasive' authority which will vary with the reputation of the writer. But the courts are more and more prepared these days to cite with approval relevant passages from major modern textbooks. The practice of conveyancers—lawyers whose business it is to draw up conveyances, wills, and other legal documents—is sometimes valuable as evidence of what the law is.

8. *Delegated powers of legislation*

In many cases Parliament has conferred by statute on government departments, on public officers, and on public bodies such as local government authorities, the power of making by-laws, rules, or regulations for definite purposes and within prescribed limits; and the exercise of such a power produces rules of law which are equivalent in force to statutory enactment. In recent times Parliament has been very lavish in giving such powers to government departments—in some cases a government department has even been given power to modify an Act of Parliament.

A committee of judges and lawyers has power to make rules for the procedure in the High Court. In exercising this power they are genuinely legislating. They are not bound by precedent, but make such rules as they think proper.

2   Common law and equity

1. *Equity and morality*

Apart from Common Law and Statute Law, the most important department of our legal system is Equity. We sometimes use the term 'equity', or words corresponding to it, in popular language as if it was something altogether outside law. We speak of a judgment in a particular case or of a rule laid down in a judgment as being undoubtedly according to law, but as being 'unfair', or 'unjust', or 'inequitable'. In cases of this sort we are really passing a moral judgment upon the law. Such a moral judgement in no way affects the law. It may be a reason why the law should be altered by statute; it does not prevent it from being law, or affect its operation, as long as no alteration in the law is made by statute. But when a modern lawyer uses the terms 'law' and 'equity' he does not mean to say that equity is not law. He is speaking really of two different kinds of law—the Common Law on the one side, the rules of Equity on the other—which are equally law. They are rules which are not merely morally but legally binding: they are enforced by the courts.

2. *The relation between law and equity*

(1) The distinction between law and equity occurs in other systems. Thus the *ius honorarium*, developed by the praetor's edict, played a vital part in the development of Roman Law. But while in Rome *ius honorarium* was administered in the same courts as the *ius civile*, in England law and equity, until the Judicature Act 1873 came into effect in 1875, were administered in different courts.

(2) These two sets of rules, though distinct, must not be looked upon as two co-ordinate and independent systems. On the contrary, the rules of Equity are only a sort of supplement or appendix to the Common Law; they assume its existence but they add something further. In this way Equity is an *addendum* to the Common Law.

(3) Further, the rules of Equity, though they did not contradict the rules of Common Law, in effect and in practice produced a result opposed to that which would have been produced if the Common Law rules had remained alone. A Common Law right was practically, though not theoretically, nullified by the existence of a countervailing equitable right. In this sense we may speak of a 'conflict or variance' between the rules of Law and the rules of Equity, in the language of section 25 (sub-section 11) of the Judicature Act 1873 (now replaced by section 49 of the Supreme Court Act 1981).

(4) Though since the Judicature Act came into force in 1875 the rules of Common Law and Equity are recognized and administered in the same court, yet they still remain distinct bodies of law, governed largely by different principles. In order to ascertain the rights to which any given set of facts give rise, we must always ask (i) what is the rule of Common Law? (ii) what difference (if any) is made in the working of this rule by the existence of some rule of Equity applying to the case?

(5) Like the Common Law, the rules of Equity are judicial law, i.e. to find them we must look in the first instances to the decisions of the judges who have administered Equity. But some branches of Equity, like some branches of the Common Law, have been restated with amendments and additions in codifying Acts, such as the Partnership Act 1890.

3. *History*

At the end of the thirteenth century we find three great courts definitely established: King's Bench, Common Pleas, Exchequer.

All are King's Courts, as opposed to the Communal Courts of counties and hundreds, Lord's Courts, or Ecclesiastical Courts. Each has its proper sphere, but in course of time each of them extends its jurisdiction, so that the same matters may often be dealt with indifferently by any one of them. All these three administer substantially the same law, which, by the time of Edward I, is already called Common Law, because it is a law common to the whole of England; and it is becoming a fairly definite body of rules, capable of growth and expansion in various directions, but still with well-marked boundaries which cannot be transgressed. These courts continued to exist until 1875, and are known as the Common Law Courts.

Standing outside these courts is the Chancellor. He is not originally a judge, nor has he a court. He is the head of a great Government office—what may be called the secretarial office. The legal historian Maitland called him 'the King's Secretary of State for all departments'. Whatever writing has to be done in the King's name is done by the Chancellor or through him and his officers.

In one way the Chancellor is already brought into relation with the administration of justice, though not so as to enable him to modify the law at his pleasure. The writs, i.e. the King's commands that a person shall appear in one of the King's Courts in answer to a claim, are issued in his name, as they still are today, and are issued from his office. Many writs are already framed and well recognized to meet the cases that usually arise; you can have them for the asking, if you pay the fee.

The question whether a man who considers himself wronged has a claim which he can make good will depend on the answer to the question: Is there a writ to meet his case or, if there is not one, can one be framed which the King's Courts will hold good? The Chancery, i.e. the Chancellor's office, has a power (Statute of Westminster II 1285) of framing new writs *in consimili casu*—i.e. to meet new cases sufficiently like those for which writs already exist—and new writs are from time to time framed. But here the Common Law Courts manage to get the last word; for they acquired the power, in the fifteenth century, to decide whether the writ is good or not and, if not, the fact that the plaintiff has got the writ will not help him. In deciding whether a writ is good or not the judges will be guided by the already accepted Common Law principles. Now it will sometimes happen that the working of the law and procedure of the Common Law Courts will result in particular cases in injustice and hardship. *We* might feel inclined to say: Well, that is a pity, but it would be a greater evil to interfere; it would be worse to make the law uncertain than to leave a particular hardship unredressed. That was not the way that our ancestors looked at the matter. Law and morality were not yet clearly distinguished, nor could one even say that the whole of law or justice was to be found in any one court. The Ecclesiastical Courts, and Local Courts of many different kinds, administered a justice which was not the justice of the Common Law Courts; so the thought was natural that even the King's justice was not exhausted in the power conferred on his courts. A reserve of justice remained with the King, and so those who could not get relief in the King's ordinary courts might, with some hope of success, petition the King and his Council for redress, if not as a matter of right at least as a favour. These petitions in practice were referred to the Chancellor, who was the chief minister and secretary and the most learned member of the King's Council. In course of time these petitions came to be addressed direct to the Chancellor himself.

Putting aside what does not concern us here, cases where the petitioner asked for redress against the King himself, we may note two kinds of cases where this extraordinary relief is asked for:

(1) Where the petitioner has suffered an undoubted legal wrong—been assaulted and beaten, or turned out of his property—but for some reason cannot get redress, because he is poor and his opponent is rich and powerful, because juries are corrupt or timid. In this class of cases redress was given in the Middle Ages sometimes by the King's Council and sometimes by the Chancellor. In the sixteenth and early seventeenth centuries

this jurisdiction was abandoned by the Chancellor and passed to the Court of Star Chamber. When the Court was abolished in 1641 the Common Law Courts had become strong enough to give adequate redress.

(2) Cases of transactions which give, at any rate, a moral right, but a right which the Common Law Courts cannot or will not protect. In particular we find the cases of what are called 'uses' or trusts—transactions whereby a man legally transfers land to another, but with an understanding that the transferee will hold it for the benefit of the former, or for the benefit of those whom he will name in his will. The Common Law has already very strict notions as to the kinds of rights in land which it will protect, and the methods of transfer which it will allow. Uses and trusts the Common Law will not recognize; wills of land, it has decided, are void (unless established by local custom—it was not until 1540 that a statute was passed giving power to leave land by will). But the practice of creating these uses and trusts was popular and was growing, and the absence of all legal protection for them was a great hardship. So we find, by the end of the fourteenth century, that persons are directing petitions to the Chancellor, claiming that they have at least a moral right to the benefit of these uses, and begging him to give them help against the legal owner who is setting up his Common Law rights against them.

Now the Chancellor is at this time usually an ecclesiastic, commonly a bishop, and, as such, interested in, and, at least in his own opinion, a good judge of questions of morality or 'conscience'. He is commonly spoken of as the keeper of the King's conscience. What can he do to help the humble suppliant? He cannot interfere directly with the proceedings of the Common Law Courts; he cannot issue a new writ which will have much chance of being held good by those courts. But he can do this: he considers the petition, or Bill, as it is called; if he thinks there is anything in the case, he issues a writ which requires the person complained against to appear, not in a Common Law Court, but before himself, and answer the petition on oath. The writ is called a *subpoena*, because it requires him to appear upon pain of forfeiting a sum of money.

When the defendant comes before the Chancellor, he will have to answer the Bill on oath. This is very different from the Common Law procedure, which will never compel, or even allow (at that time), one of the parties to an action to give evidence; but it is a procedure, and the only procedure, which is suitable for trying such questions as uses and trusts, for which no open public acts, no formal documents may be available as evidence. So, too, the Chancellor tries the whole case himself; he does not—as must be done in Common Law cases—send it to be tried by a jury. It is true that in later times particular questions arising in a case before him, suitable for trial by jury, are sometimes directed by the Chancellor to be so tried.

Suppose now that the Chancellor has decided in favour of the petitioner, and has held that the land which legally belongs to the defendant ought to belong, or, 'in conscience', in equity, morally, does belong to the petitioner. What will he do? He cannot reverse the rule of Common Law; he cannot interfere—at least directly—with proceedings in the Common Law Court; he cannot say that the legal owner is *not* the legal owner. What he can do is say that the legal owner cannot in conscience, in equity, make use of his Common Law right for his own benefit; he must use it for the benefit of the man for whom he holds it in trust. He does not stop at saying so. He can, if the legal owner will not act as equity and conscience dictate, punish him, if necessary, by putting him in prison. He can even indirectly, but effectively, interfere with the legal owner's attempts to enforce his legal rights by action in the Common Law Courts. He cannot forbid the Common Law Courts to try an action; but he can forbid a man to bring it, or to go on with it, or to take advantage of the judgment which he has got, and can put him in prison if he does not obey. He has the less scruple in issuing such orders because he can say that he is really doing what is in the man's own highest interest. If he is doing what is against conscience, he is injuring his soul—remember that the Chancellor is an ecclesiastic—and it is better that he should be prevented from inflicting such injury on himself.

This sort of interference, which had started as a matter of special favour in special cases, gradually becomes a regular practice. It becomes popular; uses and trusts become part of the ordinary machinery by which people deal with their property; they even lend themselves to abuse, which has to be checked by Acts of Parliament in the fourteenth, fifteenth, and sixteenth centuries. The Chancellor develops what in effect is, and comes to be known as, a court—the Court of Chancery. And then that general principle of Equity, which began as the mere application of moral sense to particular cases, develops into more and more definite rules. If a Chancellor has decided that certain conduct in one case is against conscience, he is likely to decide that similar conduct is against conscience in another: the chances are that another Chancellor will decide the same. You get what in reality is a new set of rules of law—rules which you can rely on as likely or certain to be applied uniformly in the future. And you get a new set of rights—rights which can be enforced in the Chancellor's Court side by side with the Common Law rights, which alone can be enforced in the Common Law Courts, the former in effect, though not in theory, overriding the latter. You even get to think of two sorts of ownership. From saying that a thing ought to belong to a man, that it ought to be used for his benefit, you come to saying that it actually *is* his, 'in equity' or 'in conscience'.

A few points in the development of Equity may now be noted.

In 1535 Henry VIII struck a blow at uses in the Statute of Uses. The King's main object in forcing the Act through Parliament was to regain the revenue from the perquisites enjoyed by a feudal lord and paid or owed by his tenants, known as the incidents of feudal tenure[1] which had been depleted by the practice of conveying land to uses (see below, Chapter 5). The statute enacted that where A was seised (i.e. possessed) of a freehold interest in land, to the passive use that he allow B to enjoy the land, B's equitable interest should be turned into a legal interest. The result was that in these cases the separation between legal and equitable ownership ceased. But this separation still continued in the cases to which the statute did not apply—e.g. if the trustee had active duties to perform, or if he was possessed, not of a freehold, but of chattels real or personal to another's use. Moreover the effect of the statute, in preventing the separation between legal and equitable estates in the cases to which it applied, was nullified in the latter half of the seventeenth century by the decision of the Chancery to protect trusts declared upon the uses which the statute had turned into legal estates. If X gave land to A to the use of B, B got the legal estate by the Statute of Uses; but if X gave land unto and to the use of B in trust for C, B was the legal owner of the land and C the equitable owner. Thus, under the name of trusts, equitable rights in land grew up again and flourished.

From the Reformation onwards the Chancellor was usually a layman: Bishop Williams under James I and Charles I was the last clerical Chancellor. Again the Chancellor comes to be usually a lawyer: Lord Shaftesbury under Charles II was the last Chancellor who had never been a practising lawyer. All this tends to create a more definitely legal character for the rules of Equity.

Meanwhile Equity is adding new fields of jurisdiction. In the sixteenth century and the beginning of the seventeenth, *fraud* and *accident*—especially the accidental loss of a document—are regarded as matters peculiarly appropriate for relief in a Court of Equity—matters which a Common Law Court cannot sufficiently deal with. Mortgages form a special subject which the Chancellor deals with. A man borrows money and transfers his land to the creditor, making the creditor legally owner. He promises to pay on a definite date. If he keeps his promise, his land is to be returned to him; if not, it is to belong to the creditor for ever. Suppose by mistake or accident he fails to repay on the day named, is it fair that he should be held to the terms of the deed? Equity says no, and soon goes so far as to lay down a rule that a mortgage is a mere security for money, and something quite different from a genuine transfer of the ownership. The debtor remains in a sense owner; he has a new sort of equitable ownership, 'an equity of redemption', which he is only to lose after the court has given him ample opportunity to repay, and it becomes plain to the court that he cannot or will not pay.

In the seventeenth century the Chancery had to struggle for its independence against the Common Law Courts. They resented the way in which the Chancellor interfered—in effect though not in theory—with their judgments, by prohibiting the man who was successful at Common Law from putting them into force. A great quarrel broke out between Chief Justice Coke and Lord Ellesmere, the Chancellor: it was decided by King James I in favour of the latter. Under the Commonwealth there were proposals for reforming, and even abolishing, the Chancery. Its extraordinary jurisdiction in civil matters was compared with the extraordinary jurisdiction of the now defunct Star Chamber in criminal matters. These proposals came to nothing. Somewhat similar proposals at the time of the Revolution of 1688, for subjecting the Chancery to the control of the Common Law Courts, were rejected. It was clear that Chancery was doing work which the Common Law Courts could not or would not do, and without which men's rights could not be sufficiently protected. Equity had come to stay as part of the law of the land.

The work increases. The Master of the Rolls, who is originally a very subordinate officer, with charge of the documents of the court, comes to be at the end of the seventeenth century a judge who can hear Equity cases, though there is an appeal from him to the Chancellor. For a long time these two between them do most of the Equity work, though the Court of Exchequer has also developed an Equity jurisdiction, an 'Equity side', which, however, is handed over to Chancery in 1842: it is now administered by the Queen's Bench Division of the High Court. The work of the court was too much for the judges; and this cause of delay was aggravated by the dilatory character of the procedure, and by the time which some of the Chancellors took to consider their decisions. At the beginning of the nineteenth century we find Lord Eldon sometimes keeping a case for ten years to think over, and not delivering judgment until perhaps most of the parties were dead and most of the property had gone in costs. Early in the nineteenth century additional judges, called Vice-Chancellors, were appointed—first one, later three; and a Court of Appeal in Chancery, intermediate between the Vice-Chancellors and the House of Lords, was established in 1851. The old dilatory procedure was reformed in 1852. The Chancellor gradually retired from acting as judge of first instance, and reserved himself for the Court of Appeal in Chancery and for the House of Lords.

Finally, the Judicature Acts in 1873–5 abolish the old Court of Chancery, as they abolish the Common Law Courts and certain other courts, and establish a new court—the High Court of Justice—which has all the powers of a Court of Common Law and a Court of Equity, and in which both sets of rules, the rules of Law and the rules of Equity, are administered; but in which, if there is 'conflict or variance' between them, the rules of Equity are to prevail. The court has now three divisions: a Queen's Bench Division, a Chancery Division, and a Family Division (successor to the Probate, Divorce, and Admiralty Division, of which something will be said in Chapter 3). The Queen's Bench and Chancery Divisions are no longer distinct courts, though, as a matter of working convenience, matters which involve mainly the Common Law come before the Queen's Bench; those which largely involve Equity come before the Chancery Division. But there is no hard and fast line: a plaintiff will often have a choice in which division he will start his action, and the rules of Law and Equity are equally applied in both.

4. *The main spheres of modern equity*

Before discussing the effect which the Judicature Acts have had in combining Law and Equity in one court, it will be convenient to note some of the branches of Law in which Equity has made important additions to the Common Law and done work which the Common Law could or did not do.

First in the law of property. The trust is still with us. We make settlements by which we provide that property shall devolve from one person to another within the limits which the law allows, e.g. to a man, then to his wife, then to be divided among his children. Before 1926, if we were dealing with *real* property in the strict sense, i.e. freeholds and copyholds, it is true that the trust was not necessary. Common Law allowed us to cut up a freehold estate into successive estates, each recognized by Common Law. But we shall see that, since 1925, this is not possible (see p. 97), so that the only way in which future interests in any kind of property can be created is through the machinery of a trust. So with mortgages. Until 1926 we had not invented a way of mortgaging property without creating equitable interests. Before 1926, either the debtor conveyed the legal right to a mortgagee, and retained an equitable interest—the 'Equity of Redemption'—or else he retained the legal right himself, and gave an equitable interest to the lender, as by a deposit of title-deeds. The latter form of mortgage is still possible; but, instead of the former, a form of mortgage has been invented under which both mortgagor and mortgagee take legal estates (see pp. 108–11).

Very characteristic in connection with these equitable interests is the doctrine of notice, or, more fully, the doctrine that an equitable interest is good against everyone who gets hold of the property, unless he has the legal ownership and acquired the property for value without notice, i.e. without knowledge of, and without reason to suspect, the existence of the equitable interest. At the present day, however, the rights of the purchaser of the legal estate for value without notice are diminished by the Land Charges Act 1972, which has in certain cases prevented such a purchaser from defeating the rights of the equitable owners, by enabling certain rights in the land to be registered, and providing that registration is equivalent to notice. Common Law knows next to nothing of notice. At Common Law either you have got no rights at all, or you have rights which are good against everyone, notice or no notice. That doctrine of notice has got into the Common Law in one or two places, e.g. in the law of negotiable instruments; but, broadly speaking, whenever you have got rights which depend upon notice, you may be pretty sure that you are in the sphere of Equity.

Then as regards contracts. Notice first the doctrine of undue influence. Common Law treated a contract as voidable if made under duress, i.e. threats of violence to life or limb; it took no account of more subtle forms of pressure—the unfair advantage taken of a man in distressed circumstances, the influence exercised in certain relations, such as that of a guardian and his former ward, or solicitor and client. But Equity treated such pressure as a ground for holding the transaction voidable. It would not allow it to be enforced against the promisor; and if property had been transferred, the recipient was treated as holding it for the benefit of the person who had parted with it, and as bound to restore it. So in the case of fraud and misrepresentation Equity interfered, though Common Law took account of them too. It is not clear that the rules in Common Law and Equity were quite the same on these subjects; but, at any rate, Equity had a special protection for the party who had suffered. Common Law might enable the defrauded party to resist an action brought against him on the contract; Equity could order the document to be handed up and destroyed or cancelled. That might be a necessary protection in order, e.g., to prevent a cheque obtained by fraud from getting into the hands of an innocent holder, who would be in better position than the original party to the fraud. So, too, Equity might order a document executed under a mistake to be rectified; Common Law would at most treat it as void.

Then there are the rules about time and penalties. Common Law would treat a provision in a contract as to time as being 'of the essence of the contract', meaning that if a certain act was not done by one party within a certain stipulated time, he should lose all rights under the contract; Equity treated such a provision in general as not being of the essence of the contract, but as giving a right only to damages. Again where a contract provides, e.g., that A shall pay £100 on 1 January next, and, if he does not do so, shall pay £200, Equity would not allow the £200 to be claimed, but treated it only as a security for the £100 with interest. The equitable rules about penalties were, however, to a large extent already introduced into the Common Law Courts by statutes passed at the end of the seventeenth and early in the eighteenth century.

Again, we have the rules about the assignment of rights under contract. A owes money to B. Common Law regards this as purely a relation between A and B. B agrees with C that C shall have the right to claim the debt from A. Common Law pays no attention, C cannot claim the debt. The most that can be done is that B may allow C to use his name to claim the money. But Equity treats the debt as transferable. It will compel B to let C make the legal claim in his name; in the last resort it might allow C to take proceedings in Equity in his own name against A. Thus it came to be said that 'in Equity debts and choses in action are assignable'.

Further, we must notice the law about married women. Common Law put the wife, both as regards rights and liabilities, in a very subordinate position to her husband. Her tangible movable goods simply became her husband's property. Debts due to her might be collected by the husband; and if that was done, of course the money was his. If he did not collect it, and the wife survived him, the claim for the debt remained hers. Her freehold and copyhold land, it is true, remained her own; but the husband had the enjoyment of it at least during the continuance of the marriage. Neither could dispose of the inheritance without the consent of the other. Leaseholds were in a position very much like debts. The husband had a right to dispose of them for his own benefit while he lived, and his wife had no power of disposition during that time, though, if she survived him, and they had not been disposed of, they would be hers again. Further, no married woman could make a will without her husband's consent, nor (with trifling exceptions) make any contract, except as agent either for her husband or for some other person: it would have been absurd to let her contract when she had no free property out of which she could pay. But then about the end of the seventeenth century Equity invented the separate use for married women. Property might be given to a trustee upon trust for the separate use of the married woman, free from the control and liabilities of her husband. Now, if it had simply been given to the woman, Common Law would have said, 'We can pay no attention to this separate use. If it is the woman's, it comes under the husband's control, in spite of anything you say to the contrary.' But then the property was not given to her; it was given on the face of it to the trustee. Common Law could not prevent the trustee employing it for the wife's benefit, and Equity would compel him to do so. And then Equity went one step further. Suppose a man who knows nothing of trusts and trustees, but has heard something of the separate use, leaves property—say £1,000—to his married daughter 'for her separate use'. The husband pounces on it; the Common Law makes it his. But Equity will not be baulked. True, the £1,000 belongs to the husband at law—there is no denying it; but Equity will compel him to apply it for the wife's benefit. Has not the testator, in fact, declared a trust in saying 'for her separate use'? Nothing easier than to turn the husband into a trustee for his own wife. And so this property held for the wife's separate use comes to be her 'separate estate' in Equity. Equity treats her as if she was the unmarried owner of it; it lets her dispose of it as she pleases in her lifetime, it lets her leave it by will, it even lets her make contracts which can be enforced against it, and against it only. And then Equity gets afraid of what it has done. If the wife can so easily dispose of this property, it may be that her husband will coax or bully her into parting with it to him or to his creditors, and so it allows her a privilege which no other grown-up person of sound mind in the country can enjoy. The will or settlement may impose the restraint on anticipation. In that case, no act of the married woman is to affect her right to the capital or future income of the property. It is just because the whole of this institution of married women's property existed in Equity only that Equity could mould the institution just as it pleased. Thus it was through Equity that a married woman acquired a limited and special capacity to own property and to make contracts. We shall see that in the nineteenth century this limited and special capacity was extended with some modifications to all married women (see pp. 56–60); but that in 1935 it was swept away, and married women were given the same capacity to own property and make contracts as a man.

And then, finally, look at what Equity can do for the successful plaintiff—the 'remedy', the 'relief' which it can give him. With few exceptions the only thing that Common Law can do is to give him *money* compensation. If you have been wrongfully turned out of your land, then, it is true, Common Law will put you back into possession; but this is practically the only exception from the rule that the Common Law remedy for every wrong and every breach of contract is *damages*. With the one exception mentioned, Common Law will not order a defendant to do anything except pay money. It is a much easier order to enforce. It is easier to say whether a man has paid the money or not than to say whether he has complied with other orders; and if he fails to pay, it is easy to get the money by selling his goods, if he has any. But it is not always satisfactory to the plaintiff. It may not be money that he wants; and even if he would be satisfied with money, it may be very hard to say what would be a fair compensation for his loss, and a jury may not be the most suitable body for assessing it. Suppose a contract for the sale of land; the seller refuses to perform it. In the eye of the Common Law there is plenty of land as good elsewhere; but the purchaser has set his heart on just this piece of land, and damages (even if liberally assessed, which is not always the case) are not what he wants. Or suppose the purchaser backs out. It may be of vital importance to the seller to get the money instead of the land; but he will rarely succeed in getting more than his out-of-pocket expenses. Or suppose, again, that your neighbour has agreed with you that he will not open a public house or carry on a school of music next door, and does and threatens to continue doing one or the other; or that you have a right to light for your windows, and he threatens to erect a building within three feet of them. In all such cases you may not be satisfied to receive even large damages for the wrong done; and what the amount of damages is to be may be very uncertain. At any rate, if damages are the only thing to be got, your wealthy neighbour might buy the right to annoy you. It was to meet cases of this kind that

Equity invented the great remedies of *specific performance* and *injunction*: specific performance to compel a man actually to do what he has promised—to give you the land in return for the money, to pay you the purchase money in return for the land; injunction to forbid him to do what he has promised not to do or what he has no right to do—to forbid him to open the public house or the music-school, to forbid him to build so as to block up your light, even to compel him to pull down the objectionable wall; the last sort of injunction is called *mandatory*.

5. *The effect of the Judicature Acts*

Now, what have the Judicature Acts 1873 and 1875 done?

(1) It may be noted that these acts were replaced by the Supreme Court of Judicature (Consolidation) Act 1925, which has itself now been replaced by the Supreme Court Act 1981, and by certain provisions in the Limitation Act 1980 (consolidating earlier Limitation Acts).

(2) They have established a single court with all the powers both of a Court of Law and a Court of Equity. The distribution of work between the divisions of that court is only a matter of convenience; the Queen's Bench Division can never say 'here a matter of Equity is involved; we cannot decide it', or the Chancery Division 'this is a question of Common Law; you ought to have gone to a Common Law Court'. At the worst the plaintiff who starts in the wrong division will be removed to another division, and may have to pay the expenses, if any, incurred by his mistake; but he cannot fail altogether for his mistake.

(3) Multiplicity of proceedings is avoided. Suppose a dispute about a piece of land. A is the legal owner; B has an equitable claim. Under the old system A takes proceedings in the Common Law Courts to establish his rights; B has no legal defence; he must go to the Court of Chancery to get, among other things, an injunction to forbid A to go on. Under the Judicature Acts no injunction can be granted by one division of the court against

proceedings in another division; but in every branch of the court an equitable right may be directly asserted and may be pleaded as a defence to a legal claim. So, again, suppose A is blocking up B's light. Under the old system B might have had to bring two actions against A: in the Common Law Courts to get damages, in the Chancery to get an injunction to forbid the continuance of the building. He can now get both in the same action, because the same court can both give damages and also grant an injunction. Or suppose that A has broken his contract to sell land to B; here, again, B might have had to bring one action in a Common Law Court for damages, and another in the Chancery to compel specific performance. Or, again, A has a purely legal claim against B; but in order to prove his case he wants to make B disclose facts or documents which support A's claims. There A would have had to take proceedings for 'discovery' against B in Chancery to get the disclosure, and another action in the Common Law Courts for his actual claim. He now brings an action in the High Court, in the course of which he gets an order for discovery, B is compelled to disclose the documents which he has that support A's case, and A may be allowed to administer interrogatories to B—questions in writing which B must answer also in writing but upon oath.

(4) On the other hand, the old Chancery practice which compelled B to go through the whole of A's story and give an answer upon oath to everything said in it has disappeared; the evidence in the ordinary course is given *viva voce* in court when the trial comes on.

(5) The Acts introduced a whole code of procedure, the Rules of the Supreme Court, which in various ways assimilated the Common Law and the Equity procedure, taking the good points of both.

(6) The 25th section of the Act of 1873 dealt specially with a number of points in which there was a difference between Law and Equity, of which the following may here be mentioned:

(*a*) Mortgages. Common Law treated the mortgagee as the owner of the land in case of the ordinary legal mortgage; Equity treated the mortgagor as still being in a sense owner. It is true that it would not prevent the mortgagee taking possession, though it made his position in some degree uncomfortable if he did take possession. But suppose that, as usually happens, the mortgagor is left in possession, and that a stranger turns him out, or tries to do so. Common Law found a difficulty in protecting him against the stranger. The mortgagee would have to be joined as plaintiff. The Judicature Act decided that as against a stranger the mortgagor in possession must be treated as owner. He can sue in his own name. We shall see that the Law of Property Act 1925 has changed the form of the ordinary legal mortgage (see pp. 108–11). But the same rules as before are applicable to a mortgagee who takes possession, and to a mortgagor who is in possession.

(*b*) Assignment of debts and choses in action. Here you remember that Common Law would not recognize the assignment; Equity in effect would, by compelling the assignor to lend the use of his name to the assignee for the purpose of suing the debtor, or, in the last resort, allowing the assignee to sue directly against the debtor, but requiring him, as a rule, to make the assignor a defendant. Here the Judicature Act made a definite alteration in the law. It left the old equitable assignment untouched, and it may be used still. But it created a new kind of assignment, which was a legal assignment in the sense that the assignee might sue directly in his own name without making the assignor a party; but it made certain special requirements: (1) the assignment must be absolute, (2) it must be in writing, (3) notice in writing to the debtor is required. (This series of provisions in the Judicature Act is repealed and substantially re-enacted in section 136 of the Law of Property Act 1925.) None of these requirements applies to an equitable assignment, but priority as between two assignees of the same debt depends on priority of notice to the debtor, and for this purpose an unwritten notice is unavailing. On the other hand, the new kind of assignment resembles the equitable assignment in being subject to equities, i.e. to claims or defences which the debtor or other person might have set up against the assignor.

(*c*) The rules of Equity as to stipulations about time and other provisions, which would not be held by Equity to be of the essence of the contract, are to prevail in all cases.

(7) Finally, the 25th section (now substantially re-enacted by section 49 of the Supreme Court Act 1981) contains a general provision that in all other matters where there is a conflict or variance between the rules of Law and the rules of Equity the latter are to prevail. This last provision looks so sweeping that there is a danger of supposing that it has swept away all difference between legal and equitable rights. That would be a great mistake. One might imagine, for instance, that it has turned equitable estates and rights into legal estates and rights. That is not so. The great characteristic of equitable estates, namely that they will be destroyed if the legal estate gets into the hands of a purchaser for value without notice, still holds good. A is a trustee of property for B, i.e. A has a legal right which he is bound to use for B's benefit; B is said to have an equitable right to it or an equitable estate in it. Since the Judicature Act, just as much as before it, if A sells the property to C, who knows nothing of the trust, and transfers the legal ownership to him, B's rights to the property are destroyed; he can only look to A for compensation for the breach of trust. Or, again, one might suppose that this section has extended equitable doctrines to cases to which Equity did not apply them, because they formerly never came into a Court of Equity. One might suppose that, since they now come into a court with an equitable jurisdiction, the equitable doctrine must be applied. We shall see that Law drew a clear distinction between innocent and fraudulent misrepresentation. The latter was regarded as a tort, for which an action for damages was available. But damages could not normally be obtained for an innocent misrepresentation. Equity regarded the distinction as of less importance, in the sense that if a representation were untrue, whether to the knowledge of its maker or not, and were a material factor in inducing another party to enter into a contract with him, that party was entitled to rescind the contract if he were plaintiff, or resist specific

performance if he were defendant. The passage of the Judicature Act tempted some people to think that damages might now be obtained for innocent misrepresentation. But the impression was soon shown to be erroneous. Apart from fraud, and certain exceptional cases, damages could be obtained only if the representation were fundamental, so as to constitute a condition, or must be ranked as a warranty, collateral to the main contract, such as a statement concerning the soundness of a horse. However, the Law Reform Committee in 1962 recommended that courts should be permitted to award damages, at their discretion, in all cases involving innocent misrepresentation. This was substantially enacted by the Misrepresentation Act 1967 (see also pp. 139–40), and now the court may treat a contract as still subsisting despite the existence of innocent misrepresentation, and award damages to the injured party, instead of rescinding the contract.

The general result of the fusion of Law and Equity has been, then, not to alter substantive law, but rather to alter and simplify the procedure. In order to find out what the substantive law is, we must still go back to the time when Law and Equity were administered in different courts; we may still have to picture to ourselves distinct proceedings taken about the same matter in those courts, and work out the result of those separate proceedings. Yet signs are not wanting that the mental effort of doing so is one which will become more and more difficult as the memory of the distinct courts of Law and Equity dies out; and perhaps already the unified jurisdiction of the High Court, and the statutes which have codified certain branches of Common Law and Equity, have produced some results which could hardly have been given by any combination of proceedings in the separate courts, or by the development of the law solely by means of cases decided in them.

3　Other bodies of English law

There are three other main bodies of English law: Probate, Divorce, and Admiralty, which were developed in jurisdictions distinct from the Common Law Courts and the Court of Chancery. (It is not intended in this book to deal specially with the law administered in the modern Employment Appeal Tribunal or other specialist tribunals.) In these other bodies of law we see more influence of foreign law than elsewhere in our legal system.

1. *The church courts*

From William the Conqueror onwards the Church Courts are separated from the Lay Courts: the Bishop has his court; the Archbishop a superior or prerogative court; from him before the Reformation there is an appeal to the Pope. The law of these courts is the Church or Canon Law—the Common Law of the Western Church. That law was formed by ecclesiastical lawyers who knew the Roman Law. It was first systematized by Gratian of Bologna in the twelfth century. It was the law of the Church in England, as in other parts of Western Europe, though within limits local and provincial variations were possible. Though these courts were in no sense treated as subordinate by the King's Courts, the latter would issue prohibitions to prevent them from dealing with matters that did not concern them. But the scope of their actual and proper jurisdiction was large. With a great part of the matters with which they dealt we have not much concern. Their exclusive claim to punish clergymen for ordinary offences has long since disappeared; the power to try and punish laymen for immorality has become practically obsolete; their jurisdiction over the matters of ritual, and ecclesiastical offences of clergymen, such as heresy, still remains and is still exercised by them. In the struggle between them and the King's Courts for jurisdiction over ecclesiastical property—the right to present a clergyman to a living, for instance—the King's Courts were successful at an early time in getting and keeping the jurisdiction in their own hands. But in two matters, which concern primarily what we should consider the civil rights of everyone, the Church Courts long retained their jurisdiction: the disposition of the goods of the dead, and questions of marriage and divorce.

2. *Probate and administration*

As regards the real estate of the deceased, it is settled by the end of the thirteenth century that he can make no will, except where there is a local custom to that effect. But as regards his goods and chattels, which include his leaseholds, it is early admitted that he has at least a limited power to dispose by will—limited because his wife and children may have rights which he cannot override. These restrictions on testation had disappeared over the greater part of England early in the fourteenth century, but they survived in the province of York until 1692, in Wales until 1696, and in London until 1724. If he makes no will we can hardly say that there is in early times any common law as to how his goods shall be divided; much or all will depend on local custom. The Common Law takes little interest in the goods, which are of far less importance, and especially of far less public importance, than the land. Now the Church has a definite interest in the goods of the deceased. The religious belief of the time requires at least a substantial part of his property to be devoted to the good of his soul. If he makes a will, as most men do, it is almost certain that he will set apart a considerable proportion for the saying of masses; if he should neglect to do so, and in the twelfth and thirteenth centuries it is regarded as almost a sin to die without making a will, the Church ought to make the provision which he has failed to make for his soul.

Thus the Church Courts assume a jurisdiction over dead men's goods. If there is a will—and wills at that time are very easy to make, mere word of mouth is sufficient—the Bishop's Court is the proper place in which it must be proved; the Bishop's Court will see that the executor carries out his duties properly. If there is no will, then the Bishop will take charge of the goods that the deceased leaves, and make a suitable disposition of them. The Bishop seems to have had a wide discretion, which was not always well exercised. Two statutes provided a remedy. In 1285 the 'Ordinary', i.e. the ecclesiastical superior who has the juris-diction, is required by statute to pay the debts of the intestate, just as the executor (i.e. the person appointed by the will to carry out the will) is required to pay them. In 1357 he is required by statute to entrust the administration of the property to the near relations of the deceased. This statute originated the office of *administrator*. The administrator is the person who, in the absence of an executor, must deal with the deceased's property, pay his debts, and make a proper division among those entitled. He receives what are called *letters of administration*, which give him the title to the property; even where there is a will, but no executor is appointed, there must be a grant of letters of administration *cum testamento annexo*, 'with the will attached'.

It is true that the Ecclesiastical Court is not the only one which deals with the goods of dead men; the executor or administrator may have to sue in the Common Law Courts to recover the claims or property of the deceased, and the deceased's creditors can sue him there. But neither the Ecclesiastical Courts nor the Common Law Courts are well adapted to settle the numerous conflicting rights of creditors, legatees, and next of kin; trusts are often involved, and during the last two centuries the most effectual and usual method of asserting a claim to or against the estate of a deceased person is to get the estate administered in Chancery. That court tells the executor or administrator what to do, or takes the whole estate under its charge and distributes it. But all this supposes that there is already a will proved, or letters of administration granted by the Ecclesiastical Court. Without probate of the will or letters of administration, neither executor nor administrator can take any steps in any other court of law, for the executor's proof of his title, and the administrator's title itself, can only be given by the Ecclesiastical Court. That court keeps the key which unlocks the estate.

The Reformation left the jurisdiction untouched; and it lasted into the middle of the nineteenth century. There were as many Probate Courts as there were dioceses, in addition to the Prerogative Courts of the two Archbishops, and a number of courts in places called Peculiars, places outside a bishop's jurisdiction, and under a special ecclesiastical jurisdiction of their own. The appropriate court was usually the court of the diocese in which the deceased's property happened to be; if there was property in several dioceses, it was necessary to apply to the Prerogative Court. The records of these numerous courts were often badly kept, and there might be damage or loss of the original wills which the courts kept under their custody. In 1857 the whole of the jurisdiction of the Ecclesiastical Courts in Probate and Administration was taken away and was vested in a new court—the Court of Probate.

The Statutes of Distribution 1670 and 1685 established a code for the distribution of the property of intestate persons modelled largely on Roman law. But until 1857 this code was subject to local customs in the province of York, in Wales, and in London which gave different rights to the wife and children. We shall see that since 1925 this code is now replaced by a new scheme of intestate succession, which applies to all the property of a deceased person (see pp. 126–8).

3. *Marriage and divorce*

This also, from an early time in the Middle Ages, fell largely into the hands of the Ecclesiastical Courts. They assume a jurisdiction to declare whether a marriage has taken place or not, whether there is any impediment which makes it void or voidable. Questions of legitimacy may also be decided by them. They grant also what is called a divorce *a mensa et thoro*, or rather what we should call a judicial separation, i.e. they release the parties from the duty of living together on grounds of cruelty or misconduct; but a divorce in the modern sense, which allows the parties to marry again, is not recognized by the medieval church in the case of any marriage which is originally valid. After the Reformation it looks for a moment as if the Ecclesiastical Courts would allow even a divorce in the modern sense; but the attempt fails, and the only way of getting a complete dissolution of marriage is by special Act of Parliament (and so the law remained, for persons domiciled in Northern Ireland, up to 1939). This Divorce Act was only allowed after proceedings had been taken both in the Ecclesiastical Courts for separation, and in the Common Law Courts for damages. The expense of the combined proceedings was enormous, and made divorce a luxury of the very rich.

Here again, in 1857, statute took away the whole of the matrimonial jurisdiction from the Ecclesiastical Courts and vested it in a new court, the Divorce Court, which was enabled to do not only everything that the Ecclesiastical Court could have done, but also what previously needed the combined efforts of the Ecclesiastical Courts, the Common Law Courts, and an Act of Parliament.

4. *Admiralty*

The Middle Ages knew a number of courts with a maritime jurisdiction, which were mainly local courts, e.g. the court of the Cinque Ports. They knew also a Law Merchant which was different from the Common Law and had an international character, a law founded on the commercial customs of merchants and seafaring men of all nations. It, too, was administered in local courts held in fairs and towns. Gradually these courts decayed, partly owing to the jealousy of the Common Law Courts, which interfered with them and extended their own jurisdiction. In the course of the seventeenth and eighteenth centuries the Law Merchant, apart from maritime law and prize law (see p. 44–5), was absorbed into the Common Law; thus the law of such matters as Bills of Exchange came to be part of the law of the land, and came to have a specially English character. On the Continent mercantile law is still regarded as something separate from the ordinary law.

The Admiral, whose office dates from the end of the thirteenth century, has at first no jurisdiction apart from the discipline of the fleet, but in the course of the fourteenth century we find him assuming a jurisdiction to punish crimes, such as piracy, committed at sea, as well as a civil jurisdiction over shipping and commercial matters. The law and procedure of his court have an international rather than a purely English character; it administers a law which is to be found in the medieval maritime codes, such as the Laws of Oleron and the so-called Law of Rhodes; in the background, as a supplementary law, is the Civil or Roman law. Its procedure is that of Roman law: the parties can be examined on oath. But the Admiralty Court also suffers from the jealousy of the Common Law. Its criminal jurisdiction is, in the sixteenth century, vested in a set of commissioners who come in practice to be invariably judges of the Common Law Courts. Its civil jurisdiction was encroached upon, as contracts made and wrongs done abroad or at sea were brought within the jurisdiction of the ordinary courts by fictions, such as the pretence that such towns as Bordeaux were within the area of, say, Cheapside, so that many international commercial transactions were considered to be purely municipal. Prohibitions were issued to prevent the Admiralty from dealing with any case that the Common Law Courts could deal with.

The result of this struggle, which lasted through the sixteenth and seventeenth centuries, was to confine the court to a very limited jurisdiction, dealing with purely maritime matters, such as salvage and damage by collision at sea. It still retained such jurisdiction, and received some increase and confirmation of it, in the nineteenth century. The Maritime Law which it administered—though it gradually became more English and less international—still retained a peculiar character. For instance, the rule of contributory negligence applicable to collisions at sea differed from that established by the common law of tort. Under the Common Law, proof that the plaintiff had been guilty of contributory negligence, and that he had the 'last opportunity' of avoiding the accident, entirely deprived him of his remedy. (This rule has, as we shall see, been altered by the Law Reform (Contributory Negligence) Act 1945; see p. 156.) Maritime Law divided the loss, at first equally, but now, under the Maritime Conventions Acts 1911, in proportion, as far as possible, to the degree of fault.

The Admiralty had from the first a 'prize' jurisdiction, i.e. a jurisdiction to determine all questions as to the ownership of ships and goods captured at sea by a belligerent. The leading principles of prize law were settled by Lord Stowell during the Napoleonic wars; and they were the basis of the prize law which was applied in the 1914–18 and 1939–45 wars.

5. *The modern courts*

The Acts of 1857 which established the Probate and Divorce Courts provided that the ordinary judge of these courts might be the same person as the Admiralty judge. Thus it was a natural step that in 1875 the Probate, Divorce, and Admiralty jurisdictions should be entrusted to a single division of the High Court. However the disparity between the three jurisdictions became marked in the course of the present century, and a reorganization was brought about by the Administration of Justice Act 1970. The Probate, Divorce, and Admiralty Division was abolished and a new Family Division of the High Court put in its place. This new Division deals with Divorce and other aspects of family law, as well as non-contentious Probate, while contentious Probate is now assigned to the Chancery Division, and Admiralty matters to the Queen's Bench Division.

4 Persons and personal relations

1. *Unborn persons*

Even before birth a human being is not without legal recognition, for the antenatal life is protected by the Infant Life Preservation Act 1929. The Irish courts have held that a child which was born deformed in consequence of an injury to its mother, caused by the fault of a railway company on whose line she was travelling, could not recover damages; but the decision turned on the view that the company, not having means of knowledge of its presence, owed no duty towards it. In England, however, the birth of many children suffering from deformities caused by their mothers having taken the new drug thalidomide prescribed by doctors during their pregnancy resulted in the enactment of the Congenital Disabilities (Civil Liability) Act 1976. Under this Act a child born alive, but suffering from a physical or mental defect as a result of something which happened before its birth, has a right of action for damages if the defendant would also have been liable in tort for what occurred to the parent if sued in time.

In the law of property a child conceived, but not yet born, will be treated as born, at any rate where it is for its advantage that it should be so treated. For instance, even a bequest to persons 'born previously to the date of my will' will include a person born within due time afterwards. But if the child is never born alive, things will remain as if it had never existed. Further, by wills and settlements, provision may be made for those who may come into existence at a future time, subject to the rule against perpetuities, which forbids any disposition which is not certain to take effect (if it takes effect at all) within lives in being and twenty-one years afterwards; but a life in being includes a person *en ventre sa mere* at the time when the will or settlement takes effect. (Certain detailed modifications of the effect of the rule against perpetuities are now enacted by the Perpetuities and Accumulations Act 1964, and in 1993 the Law Commission published a consultation paper inviting views upon whether the perpetuity rule should remain or be at least simplified.)

2. *Infants*

At birth a child enters the condition of infancy—a condition which ceases at the age of 18 years, or rather, at the first moment of the day preceding the eighteenth birthday. In what follows the term 'infant' will be used in its strict sense of a person who is in the condition of infancy as above defined. It would be a mistake to regard the condition of infancy as one of uniform incapacity throughout and for all purposes. In Criminal Law the material periods are those up to 10 and between 10 and 14 years. A child under 10 incurs no criminal liability for its acts; a child over 9, but under 14, incurs no such liability unless it is shown that it had sufficient capacity to know its act was wrong. A person above the age of 13, though under 18, does not differ in general as regards criminal liability from a person of full age, though modern legislation has made special provision for the trial and punishment of persons under 17. The Marriage Act 1949 provides that a marriage between persons either of whom is under the age of 16 is void. Marriages of persons over that age, but under 18, are completely valid; and the only check on such marriages without the consent of parents or guardians is the difficulty of getting them celebrated by the clergyman or proper officer without making a false declaration, which involves penal consequences.

There is no general rule which exempts infants from liability for 'tort', i.e. civil injury other than breach of contract or trust. An infant who damages another by carelessly running into him on his bicycle is liable just as a person of full age would be. Practically, the liability is not often of much value to the injured person, for the infant probably has no property available to satisfy it, and his parents are not liable for his acts. In two ways, however, the liability of an infant for civil wrongs is restricted. It sometimes happens that the wrong is so closely connected with a contract that the enforcement of liability for the wrong would in effect amount to an enforcement of the contract. Suppose that an infant who has hired a horse injures it by careless riding. In such a case an adult might be held liable either for breach of his contract to use proper care or for a wrong independent of the contract; an infant has been held not to be liable at all. Again some wrongs, such as fraud, in their essence involve a guilty state of mind, and in such cases the extreme youth of the wrongdoer may be inconsistent with the existence of such a state of mind.

It is in respect of property and contract that the incapacity of infancy has its most general operation. This incapacity is a one-sided one. Property (other than a legal estate in land) may be transferred, and binding promises may be made to an infant, but in general he is unable to make a binding disposition of his property or to make binding promises to others. As regards property, it should be noticed that law and practice, to a large extent, make it unlikely that property of any considerable value will come into the direct ownership of an infant. When property passes on death, it will go in the first instance to the executor appointed by will, or the administrator appointed by the court, who are charged with the duty of dealing with it and transferring it to the persons entitled (see p. 128). Similarly, under the settlements which people of property commonly make, the property will be in the hands of trustees. The infant cannot give a receipt which executors, administrators or trustees can safely take. They must therefore retain the property to which an infant is entitled until he attains full age, and meanwhile deal with it under the directions of the will or settlement or under the orders of the court. But if the trust has been created after 1925, the Trustee Act 1925 gives power to the trustees to apply the property for the maintenance and advancement of the infant. In some cases trustees may relieve themselves by transferring it into the control of the court.

Where an infant actually has in his hands tangible movable property, it would seem that he has a power of disposing of it, of which the limits—if such there are—have not been determined. It cannot be supposed, for instance, that a sale by a normal infant of his own books or minor personal effects could (in the absence of fraud or unfair dealing) be called in question. It is clear that a payment made by him for goods bought is binding, though payment could not have been enforced against him. A gift of a large sum of money by an infant was after his death held valid. But the bulk of 'property', in the modern sense of the word, is not of this kind. Equitable estates in land, which are the only interests in land which infants can now have, can only be disposed of by writing; and a writing or a sealed writing is necessary for the transfer of such things as stocks and shares, claims against debtors, and interests in property held by others upon trust. In all such cases the rule would seem to apply that the infant's acts are 'voidable'; they become binding on him only if, after attaining full age, he fails within a reasonable time to repudiate them. The rule has been relaxed so as to enable infants to make a binding settlement of their property upon marriage, but only with the sanction of the court.

Except soldiers and airmen when on active service and mariners while at sea, no infant can dispose of his property by will. But in some cases a person of the age of 16 can make what is in effect equivalent to a disposition by will: a member of a Trade Union or Friendly Society may, for instance, at that age nominate in writing a person to receive moneys payable on his death by the Union or Society.

The contracts of an infant are at Common Law voidable. But in this connection the word 'voidable' has two senses. In the case of contracts creating continuing or recurrent liabilities incident to the disposition or holding of property, such as a settlement or a leasehold tenancy, the infant, on attaining full age, becomes bound unless within a reasonable time he takes steps to repudiate liability. In all other cases—as, for instance, a sale of goods or a contract for services or a loan of money—the contract was voidable in the sense that the infant would not, on attaining full age, become liable unless he took steps to ratify it. As regards this latter class of contracts, the Infants' Relief Act 1874 very much altered the law. Contracts for the loan of money and supply of goods to infants and 'accounts stated' with infants were made altogether void, while the possibility of ratification was taken away from all those contracts which required ratification to make them binding upon him after attaining full age; and even a new promise to perform the contract, whether made upon a fresh consideration or not, could not be enforced by action. These provisions gave rise to uncertainty largely because the courts showed a marked reluctance to interpret them according to the ordinary meaning of such words as 'void', and they also gave rise to injustice because under the Common Law an infant could still sue an adult upon a contract unenforceable against himself and incapable of ratification by him.

To the general invalidity of infants' contracts the Common Law recognized the exceptions of contracts for necessaries and contracts for the infants' benefit, and these exceptions are not affected by statute. Contracts for necessaries include contracts for such goods, lodging, and instruction as are reasonably necessary for the infant, having regard to his station in life and his needs at the time of the contract. The party who supplies the infant does so at his peril; it will not avail him that he did not know he was dealing with an infant, or that he thought his position in life was such as to make the goods necessary, or that he did not know the infant was already sufficiently supplied. Of contracts for the benefit of the infant, so far as they do not coincide with contracts for necessaries, a contract for the employment of the infant, where his position in life makes employment desirable for him, is a typical case.

The unsatisfactory state of the law resulting from the Infants' Relief Act 1874 has now been remedied by the Minors' Contracts Act 1987, which is based upon recommendations of the Law Commission. The 1987 Act restores the Common Law principle to contracts for the loan of money and supply of goods to infants, and to accounts stated with infants, so that they are now voidable (but not void) or unenforceable against them. On attaining majority, or within a reasonable time thereafter, an infant may ratify a contract which is otherwise unenforceable against him or voidable at his option, and he can do this by unilateral act. Furthermore, any new agreement entered into on majority whereby the infant undertakes to repay a loan advanced during minority is valid. A guarantee of a minor's contractual obligation is also enforceable against the guarantor even if the infant's contractual obligation is unenforceable. Finally, the 1987 Act provides that where a minor has acquired property under a contract which is unenforceable against him, or which he has repudiated on the grounds of minority, he may be required by the court, when it thinks it 'just and equitable' to do so, to return the property, or else property representing that which he has acquired (without prejudice to any other remedy available to the plaintiff). In this way an infant may be compelled to provide restitution for property unfairly obtained.

3. *Parents and guardians*

In some systems of law the disability of persons under full age is helped out by the powers of the parent or guardian, who can represent the child, and, by acting on his behalf or giving concurrence to his acts, can make dispositions of his property and contracts binding on him. Of such an institution we see but the rudiments or isolated survivals in English law. Our medieval law of guardianship was concerned mainly with infants who were heirs of land; and though the 'guardian in socage'—the nearest relation of the infant to whom the infant's land cannot descend—has not been abolished, the practice of settlement and of appointing trustees in whom the land, or at least powers over it, are vested, renders rare the occasions on which the very limited powers of such or any kind of guardians can be exercised over an infant's land. At the present day they have no powers over the infant's land. A conveyance to an infant does not vest the legal estate in him, but operates only as an agreement to execute a settlement in his favour. This means that the grantor must execute a principal vesting deed and trust instrument, holding the land meanwhile as trustee for the infant. If land is given to an infant by will or conveyed to him on an intestacy the legal estate vests in the representatives of the deceased who hold it in trust for the infant. Over other property of an infant, neither parents nor guardians have now—if they ever had—any effective powers, except such as a will or settlement or an order of the court may give them; they cannot, for instance, give a valid receipt for a legacy or money payable to the child. For purposes of litigation, it is true, an infant can and must be represented by an adult, who will be called 'the next friend' of an infant plaintiff, the 'guardian *ad litem*' of an infant defendant; but such a next friend or guardian represents the infant only for the purposes of the particular lawsuit, and is not necessarily, though he is commonly, the infant's parent or general guardian.

The court's powers in regard to the protection of children are constantly revised by Parliament, and are currently contained mainly in the Children Act 1989. Broadly speaking the powers and duties of parents and guardians relate not to property, but to the care and residence of the infant's person. Under the Guardianship of Minors Act 1971, as amended by the Guardianship Act 1973 and the Domestic Proceedings and Magistrates' Courts Act 1978, both father and mother were equally entitled to the care and custody of the infant; and in case of a dispute between them the court, in coming to a decision, had to regard only the welfare of the infant. Both the 1971 and 1973 Acts have now, however, been repealed by the Children Act 1989 which makes the welfare of the child the prime consideration of the court on all occasions. Wherever possible children should be brought up and cared for within their own families, and they should be kept fully informed about what is happening to them and, if possible, should participate when decisions are made about their future. Courts should only intervene and make orders concerning, e.g. residence and parental contact if strictly necessary. Both parents must now contribute towards the welfare of their children. They are no longer seen as winning or losing over them, and the former parental rights have given way to parental responsibility. In a case in 1991 an unmarried father was granted a generous amount of contact with his 15-month-old daughter, who was to remain in residence with her mother. The following year an 11-year-old girl successfully applied to a court for a residence order to remain living with her grandparents, rather than her mother, because the judge was satisfied that this was the best course in view of her considered wishes and her objective welfare.

The Child Abduction Act 1984 makes it an offence for any parent or guardian to take or send a child out of the United Kingdom without the consent of any other person who is a parent or guardian of the child. Under the Social Security Act 1971 a man is liable to maintain his wife and children, including those of whom he has been adjudged the putative father, and a woman is liable to maintain her husband and children. Such parental responsibility can only be altered by the court, and only then if it is in the interests of the child's welfare. On the death of father or mother the guardianship devolves on the surviving spouse; but either can by deed or will appoint guardians to act with the survivor.

A natural progression from the Children Act 1989 has been the Child Support Act 1991, which introduced a new method of calculating maintenance for children, and set up the Child Support Agency to assess, collect, and enforce maintenance payments by absent parents (generally fathers). This has not been a popular measure with many of those affected, particularly absent fathers who have second families to provide for, but the Agency's jurisdiction has for many purposes replaced that of the court. Its powers are due to be extended in 1996, though it is expected that the opportunity will be taken at the same time to make a fairer apportionment of financial burden between the two parents of each child.

The court has always had power to take a child out of the residence with a parent or guardian in cases of misconduct or unfitness, and in such cases, or in the absence of any lawful guardian, to appoint a suitable person as guardian. Thus in a case in 1969, where the 10-year-old child born in England of Spanish parents had been very unhappy during the seventeen months he had spent with them in Spain, and had then lived happily for several years with foster parents and their six children in England, the court refused to make an order that care and control should be granted to the parents, one of whom was in poor health. Expert evidence was given to the effect that the chances of the child adjusting to a new life in Spain were very slim, and that failure to adjust would have very serious consequences on the child's development. The court held that the rule that the welfare of the child is to be the first and paramount consideration applies not only to disputes between parents, but also to a dispute between parents and a third party. Similarly, a parent or guardian may apply to have an infant made a ward of court if such an order would protect the infant's property from his own possible rash activities. A ward of court cannot be taken out of the jurisdiction of the court, nor can any change be made in his or her position in life, without leave of the court. Thus to marry such a ward without the consent of the court is punishable as a contempt of court. Under the Children Act 1989 the court in these matters is said to be dealing with 'care proceedings', and the term 'ward of court' should eventually disappear.

The powers of parents and guardians include the power of administering reasonable punishment, and such a power may be delegated by them to others, such as schoolmasters, under whose control the child is placed.

4. *Legitimacy*

Broadly speaking, one may say that every child is legitimate which is born during the continuance of a marriage or within due time afterwards. The presumption that the husband is the father of his wife's children is one that can be overthrown only by evidence of the most cogent, even though not of the most direct, kind. Until recently there were several legal disadvantages for anyone born illegitimate, though a series of statutes progressively reduced their number, and the Law Commission recommended the total abolition of the concept of illegitimacy. Now at last this has been achieved, first in Scotland by the Law Reform (Parent and Child) (Scotland) Act 1986, and then in England and Wales by the Family Law Reform Act 1987, with the result that in law there is now no distinction made between those born in and those born out of wedlock. Thus illegitimacy is no longer taken into consideration in determining the rights of succession of an illegitimate person, or the rights of succession to his estate, or the rights of succession traced through an illegitimate relationship. Again, illegitimate relations are included among the dependants who are entitled to claim compensation for the death of a person caused by an accident at work.

5. *Adoption*

Until 1926 English law did not recognize the institution of adoption. An Act passed in that year gave power to the court to make an adoption order. On the order being made, all the rights, duties, and obligations of the parents or guardians of the adopted child are extinguished, and these rights, duties, and obligations vest in the adopter. If a husband and wife are the adopters they have the same rights as against one another, and responsibilities for the adopted child, as if they were the child's natural father and mother. By an Act of 1934 an adopted child acquires the same rights as a natural child to benefits under what was then the Workmen's Compensation Act 1925 (now replaced by the Social Security Act 1975). By the Adoption Act 1958, property of adopter and adoptee is to devolve in all respects as if the adoptee were the child of the adopter. Finally, the Adoption Act 1968 extends the powers of courts in the United Kingdom over adoption, and enables effect to be given in the United Kingdom to adoptions made in other countries; and the Adoption Act 1976 consolidates all the earlier enactments relating to adoption.

The adopter must fulfil one of the following requirements: (*a*) be over 21; or (*b*) be the parent of the adoptee, where the other natural parent is dead, or cannot be found, or there is some other reason justifying the exclusion of the other natural parent. If a sole adopter is a male he cannot adopt a female, unless the court is satisfied that there are special circumstances which justify the adoption. Except under special circumstances the parents, guardians, or persons liable to contribute to the support of the child must give their consent to the adoption. The court must be satisfied that all persons whose consent is required understand the legal effect of the adoption. It must also be satisfied that the adopter has not received nor agreed to receive, and that no person has made or given or agreed to make or give to the adopter, any payment in consideration of the adoption, except such as the court may sanction. Other conditions may be imposed by the court as it sees fit.

6. *Married women*

Women, though at one time excluded from most public functions, were never by reason merely of their sex in a substantially different position from men as regards criminal liability, property and contract, if we except the rule, now obsolete, which used to prefer males to females in the succession to real estate on intestacy. A married woman, on the other hand, had at Common Law a very peculiar status involving both disabilities and privileges. The Criminal Justice Act 1925 abolished the presumption that an offence committed by a wife in the presence of her husband is committed under his coercion. But the rigour of the criminal law is relaxed in her favour by the provision of the same Act that, on a charge against her for any offence, other than treason or murder, it is a good defence to prove that the offence was committed in the presence of and under the coercion of her husband. She does not become criminally liable merely by assisting her husband to escape punishment for a crime which she knows him to have committed; and it is only within certain limits that husband and wife are competent, and within narrower limits that they are compellable, to give evidence against one another, in criminal proceedings. Under the Law Reform

(Husband and Wife) Act 1962, husband and wife, subject to certain discretionary powers of the court, can sue each other.

An account has already been given of the proprietary and contractual disabilities of married women at Common Law and the creation by the Court of Chancery of an equitable separate estate which a married woman could freely deal with and bind by her contracts, so far as no restraint on anticipation had been imposed, and which, in any case, she could dispose of by will. But this equitable separate estate existed only where it was created by a will or settlement, or in the comparatively rare cases where the Court of Chancery exercised its jurisdiction to compel a husband to make a settlement upon his wife. Married women of the classes in which settlements and elaborately drawn wills were unknown thus remained subject to the Common Law. When the Legislature determined to reform the Common Law rules two courses were open to it. It could either provide that all married women should hold their property as their separate property—thus giving to all married women the right to dispose of their property and to make contracts binding it which formerly could only be given to them by a will or a settlement; or it could adopt the more straightforward course of making the capacity of a married woman to own property, make contracts, and incur liability for torts the same as that of a man. In 1882 the Legislature took the first of these courses. As a result of the Married Women's Property Act 1882, and later Acts, the capacity of a married woman to own property, to make contracts, and to incur liability for torts was different from that of a man. Her property was her separate property (that is, separate from her husband, so that only a married woman could have such property) and, by means of a settlement, she could be restrained from anticipating it. By her contracts or her torts she could bind only her separate property. She could not bind herself personally, with the result that she could not be made a bankrupt, unless she was carrying on a trade.

But in 1935 the Legislature decided to take the second and more straightforward course. By Part I of the Law Reform (Married Women and Tortfeasors) Act 1935, a married woman was put into the same position as a man with respect to her proprietary and contractual capacity, and, except in relation to her husband, with respect to her liability for torts. Existing restraints upon anticipation were preserved, but even these were swept away by the Married Women (Restraint upon Anticipation) Act 1964. And, by the Married Women's Property Act 1964, any money derived by a wife from an allowance made by her husband for housekeeping purposes, or any property acquired out of it, is deemed, in the absence of any agreement between them to the contrary, to belong in equal shares to the husband and wife. The Law Commission has proposed that property (other than land, insurance policies and annuities, or property bought or transferred for business purposes) bought by either spouse for their joint use and benefit should automatically belong to both unless they agree to the contrary; and legislation to this effect is awaited.

The Matrimonial Homes Act 1967 (as amended by the Matrimonial Homes and Property Act 1981) gives a spouse who is in occupation of the matrimonial home, but does not occupy it by virtue of an estate, interest, contract, or statute, protection against eviction from the dwelling without the necessity of obtaining leave of the court. If such a spouse is not in occupation, he or she may enter and occupy the home with leave of the court. These rights are called 'rights of occupation', and where the leave of the court is necessary the court may make such orders as it thinks just and reasonable having regard to the conduct of the spouses, their needs and financial resources, the needs of the children, and all other circumstances. Rights of occupation normally only continue during the subsistence of the marriage and the existence of the other spouse's estate or interest in the home, and they amount to a charge on the other spouse's estate or interest.

In the last few years the courts have contrived in effect to extend the substance of a right of occupation to a mistress who has lived on an originally permanent basis with a man, but who has now lost her partner either through death or as a result of some form of desertion. In one case, decided in 1975, Lord

Justice James commented: 'The popular meaning of "family" in 1975 would, according to the answer of the ordinary man, include this woman as a member of the man's family.' And in another case, decided in the same year, the Court of Appeal held that a mistress was entitled to a beneficial interest in the house she had shared with her lover even though he had left it to marry another woman. It is small wonder that the practice has grown up in recent years of referring, however inaccurately, to a mistress as a 'common law wife'. By the Domestic Violence and Matrimonial Proceedings Act 1976, protection against eviction from the dwelling a mistress has shared with her lover was introduced, and a host of cases decided under the Act have proved the efficacy of this enactment to safeguard a woman's residential rights, often against physical violence by her former partner. The Law Commission has now decided to examine the whole question of the property right of unmarried cohabitants, and the law as to what should happen to that property if their relationship ends.

The husband will be presumed, in the ordinary case where husband and wife live together, and she orders goods to meet the household needs, to have authorized her to pledge his credit for that purpose, unless he has supplied her with sufficient ready money. But there is no general rule that the husband is liable for his wife's debts. The husband may, for instance, decide that the needs of the household shall be provided for by a housekeeper, and that the wife shall have no authority to contract on his behalf. And the shopkeeper who supplies goods to a married woman without inquiry is not entitled to assume that she has her husband's authority. It is only when the husband, by meeting the liabilities which his wife has incurred (whether for necessaries or not) to a particular tradesman, has 'held her out' as his agent, that the tradesman is entitled to hold the husband liable until he has received notice to the contrary. The notice sometimes published in the papers to the effect that Mr Smith will no longer be liable for his wife's debts has a much more limited operation than is generally supposed. It is unnecessary as regards persons whom the husband has not by his previous conduct induced to look to him for payment; it is ineffectual as regards those who do not happen to see the advertisement. Another risk run by the shopkeeper who deals with a married woman is that he may find that, though she has property, her husband is insolvent. In such a case, if the wife contracted as agent for her husband, and disclosed that fact to the shop, she incurs no personal liability.

Liabilities for contracts and torts incurred by a married woman before marriage are binding on her, and also on her husband to the extent of any property which he may have acquired from her, as under a marriage settlement. Torts committed by the wife during marriage render her liable, but, since 1935, impose no liability on her husband unless he has authorized or ratified them.

It can be seen that by piecemeal legislation great strides have been made towards equality between the sexes as regards legal status, rights and liabilities. Though total equality might be hard to achieve because of the biological differences between the sexes, the legislation has perhaps been rounded off by the Equal Pay Act 1970 and the Sex Discrimination Acts 1975 and 1986. Under these Acts, and with only minor exceptions, employers, educational establishments, and those who provide goods, facilities and services to the public (e.g. banks, building societies, finance houses, and landlords) commit a civil offence if they do not provide men and women with the same opportunities and services. An Equal Opportunities Commission, set up by the 1975 Act, oversees the working of the Acts: it may conduct formal investigations, and seek to enforce the law by civil proceedings.

7. *Marriage and divorce*

Historically there seems to be no doubt that the English Common Law required nothing for the celebration of a marriage beyond the declared agreement of the parties, which might take the form either of a declaration of present intention, or of a promise to marry followed by actual union. This was the general law of Western Europe in the Middle Ages, and a relic of it is to be found in the old 'marriage by cohabitation with habit and repute' which is left by the Marriage (Scotland) Act 1939 as the only possible form of irregular marriage in Scotland. The House of Lords, however, in the nineteenth century decided in an Irish case that the Common Law had always required the presence of an ordained clergyman. The question is now for England an academic one; for statutes, ranging from 1753 to 1994, have prescribed the formalities necessary for a valid marriage. A marriage must be celebrated either in the presence of a clergyman of the Church of England, or (since 1836) of a Registrar of Marriages, or (since 1898) of an 'authorized person', who is usually the minister authorized by the trustees of a Nonconformist place of worship. Two other persons must be present as witnesses. The celebration must take place between the hours of 8 a.m. and 6 p.m., and must be preceded by a publication of banns or the obtaining of a Registrar's certificate or a Bishop's or Registrar's licence, and, unless a special licence is obtained from the Archbishop of Canterbury, must take place in a recognized place of worship, a Registrar's office situate in the district in which one at least of the parties resides, or any premises approved by local authorities. This last type of venue was introduced by the Marriage Act 1994, which is a step towards allowing a marriage to be held almost anywhere. Special provisions have in any case been made for death-bed marriages, marriages at home for the housebound, marriages in prisons, hospitals and places of residential care for disabled people, and for the celebration of the marriages of members of the naval, military, and air forces and their daughters in chapels licensed by the Admiralty Board or by a Secretary of State. The marriages of Jews and of members of the Society of Friends are exempt from these provisions, and may be celebrated according to the rules of these religious bodies. Provision is made for preserving a record of every marriage celebrated in the country.

The law concerning nullity and divorce has been considerably reformed in recent years, and is now mostly governed by the Matrimonial Causes Act 1973, as amended by the Children Act 1989. A failure to conform to the legal requirements in contracting a marriage will render that marriage void. A marriage is also void on the ground of nearness of relationship if it is entered into

(1) between ascendants and descendants, e.g. parent and child, grandparent and grandchild;
(2) between brother and sister, uncle and niece, nephew and aunt;
(3) between persons who, by reason of the previous marriage of one of them, are related in a way corresponding to one of the relationships above mentioned.

Under this third prohibition, therefore, a marriage between a stepson and his stepmother was void, but the Marriage (Prohibited Degrees of Relationship) Act 1986 has provided an exception. Now a man may marry his stepmother or stepdaughter, or a woman her stepfather or stepson, provided that the younger person is aged at least 21 and has not at any time before reaching the age of 18 lived as a child of the family of the older person. The same Act permits marriages between in-laws, subject to the same provisos, and also provided that the former spouses have died. By a series of Acts ranging from 1907 to 1960 exceptions had already been made permitting a man to marry his deceased or divorced wife's sister or half-sister, his niece by marriage or his aunt by marriage; and a woman may marry her deceased or divorced husband's brother or half-brother. Under the Adoption Act 1976, a marriage between a child and one who has once adopted it is prohibited, but not a marriage between the adoptee and one of the adopter's own children. But the relations by blood or marriage of a wife are not regarded as being related to the relations of her husband: thus if A and B are two brothers and C and D two sisters, the marriage of A with C will be no bar to the marriage of B and D.

A marriage celebrated between two persons, one of whom is at the time validly married, is in any case void; and any person knowingly entering into such a marriage is guilty of bigamy. The following are also void: marriages between parties who are not respectively male and female; marriages between persons, either of whom is under the age of 16 (see p. 47); and a polygamous marriage entered into outside England and Wales, if either party was at the time domiciled in England and Wales (for domicile, see pp. 69–71). In 1985, however, the Law Commission did recommend that a marriage entered into by a man or woman domiciled in England and Wales should not be invalid merely because it is entered into under a law which permits polygamy, provided that neither party is already married. If now seems likely that this recommendation will be implemented by legislation to be enacted in the course of 1995.

The law of nullity covers not only cases where the purported marriage was void, but also those where the marriage, though initially valid, is voidable, and thus may be set aside. A marriage is so voidable if it has not been consummated because of the incapacity of either party, or because of one party's wilful refusal to consummate it; if the marriage was entered into without the consent of either party (e.g. by reason of duress, mistake, or unsound mind); if at the time of the marriage one party was suffering from mental disorder of such a kind as to render him or her unfitted for marriage, or from venereal disease; or if the wife was at the time of the marriage pregnant by some other person than her husband.

Nullity of marriage must be carefully distinguished from divorce. The effect of a decree of nullity, broadly speaking, is that the marriage is treated as if it had never existed. A petition for divorce, however, postulates the existence of a valid marriage, which the court is asked to terminate. Divorce of this kind was first introduced into English law by the Matrimonial Causes Act 1857, and from then until 1969 it was based upon the doctrine that some matrimonial offence (such as adultery or desertion) must have been committed by one spouse before the other could obtain relief. A break with this doctrine was made by the Divorce Reform Act 1969, now replaced by the Matrimonial Causes Act 1973, as amended in 1984, and the present position is that the sole ground on which a petition for divorce may be presented is that the marriage has broken down irretrievably. Such a petition may not, without the special leave of the court, be presented until one year has elapsed since the marriage.

Some link with the doctrine of the matrimonial offence has been retained by the further provision that the court may not decide that a marriage has broken down irretrievably unless the petitioner can establish one or more of the five following circumstances:

(1) that the respondent has committed adultery, and the petitioner finds it intolerable to live with the respondent;

(2) that the respondent has behaved in such a way that the petitioner cannot reasonably be expected to live with him (or her);

(3) that the respondent has deserted the petitioner for a continuous period of at least two years preceding the presentation of the petition;

(4) that the parties have lived apart for a continuous period of at least two years immediately preceding the presentation of the petition, and the respondent consents to a decree being granted; or

(5) that the parties have lived apart for a continuous period of at least five years immediately preceding the presentation of the petition.

The behaviour alleged under (1)–(3) above would amount to a matrimonial offence, while the circumstances covered by (4) amount to the first recognition in England of a right of divorce by mutual consent. Absence for seven years, coupled with the fact that a petitioner has no reason to believe that his or her spouse is alive, will enable him or her to ask the court to make a declaration that death is presumed and that the marriage is dissolved.

Although divorce is now much easier to obtain than ever before, legislation has since 1963 encouraged efforts at reconciliation. A petitioner's solicitor must now certify that he has discussed the question of reconciliation with his client, and suggested the names of suitably qualified people to help. Furthermore, resumption of cohabitation for any period up to six months is not in itself to be taken to condone the behaviour of the spouse which gives rise to the ground for divorce.

A judicial separation may be obtained upon proof of any one of the five bases for divorce mentioned above, save that there is no need to prove that the marriage has broken down irretrievably. This does not, like a divorce, enable the parties to marry again, but it releases them in other respects from the duties of married life. Upon a decree for dissolution of a marriage or judicial separation, the court may make orders for the residence, parental contact, maintenance, and education of the children, if the parents cannot agree on these matters, for financial provision to be made for the wife, and for varying marriage settlements. Separation and maintenance orders can also be obtained from magistrates' courts. The reform of the grounds for divorce has been mirrored as regards proceedings in magistrates' courts by the Domestic Proceedings and Magistrates' Courts Act 1978, a statute enacted as the result of recommendations made by the Law Commission, and since amended by the Children Act 1989, which provides that what used to be called domestic proceedings in Magistrates' Courts are now called family proceedings. Magistrates' orders may now be obtained on four grounds:

(1) that the respondent has failed to provide reasonable maintenance for the applicant;
(2) that the respondent has failed to provide, or make a proper contribution towards, reasonable maintenance for any child of the family;
(3) that the respondent has behaved in such a way that the applicant cannot reasonably be expected to live with the respondent; or
(4) that the respondent has deserted the petitioner.

The fact that divorce is in many cases equally desired by both parties makes it probable that there may in fact be some collusion between them. Collusion, which used to be a bar to divorce, is no longer prohibited, and indeed a Committee chaired by Mrs Justice Booth recommended in 1985 that the parties should in future be entitled to file joint petitions for divorce. But sometimes material facts are suppressed, or on the other hand one party may petition for divorce without the other party being aware of the proceedings. For this reason an interval of six weeks elapses between the decree *nisi*, which is made upon the hearing of the case, and the decree absolute, which finally dissolves the marriage and enables the parties to marry again, though the court has power to expedite the decree absolute in a suitable case. During this interval any person may intervene to show cause, on the ground of, e.g., the suppression of material facts, why the decree should not be made absolute, and a public officer, the Queen's Proctor, is especially charged with the duty of intervening.

It is clear that there will be further changes in the law of divorce in the next few years, though it is difficult to speculate on what they will be. In 1990 the Law Commission concluded that the law established in 1969 was confusing and unjust, that it provoked hostility and bitterness between couples, and that it could even exacerbate the effect on children of marital break-down. Accordingly, while favouring retention of irretrievable breakdown of the marriage as the sole ground for divorce, it recommended abolition of the role of fault in the law. The breakdown would need to be proved by the passage of a twelve-month minimum period of consolidation and reflection, during which couples could use conciliation, counselling, and mediation services, and they would be obliged to consider the future, and to make arrangements for children, the home, and money before being granted a divorce. The Children Act 1989 has already made shared parental responsibility for children an automatic result of divorce. In 1993 the Lord Chancellor published a consultation paper inviting views on a number of variations of this plan, and stressing the part to be played by mediation. This feature would therefore seem to be a likely component part of future divorce law reform.

8. *Insanity*

The nature and degree of insanity which will afford a defence to a criminal charge has from time to time been a matter of considerable discussion. Where the defence arises our courts will act upon the so-called 'McNaghten Rules', propounded by the judges in response to questions addressed to them by the House of Lords. An accused person is presumed to be sane, until he can prove the contrary. He will be criminally liable unless he was so insane as either 'not to know the nature and quality of the act he was doing' or 'not to know that what he was doing was against the law'. If he committed the crime under an insane delusion, his liability depends on the question whether he would have been liable had the facts been as he imagined them to be. But uncontrollable impulse, caused by mental defect, is not at present accepted as exempting from criminal liability, except that it may serve to reduce murder to manslaughter (see pp. 189–91). When a jury is satisfied that the act was committed, but that at the time the accused was so insane as not to be legally responsible, it brings in a special verdict of 'not guilty by reason of insanity', though the accused is then ordered to be detained during the 'Queen's pleasure'. Detention is usually lifelong, and for this reason insanity is not often pleaded, except very occasionally as a defence to a prosecution for murder. But even in murder cases it is now far more favourable to the accused for him to plead instead diminished responsibility, and for most practical purposes this defence has replaced that of insanity in criminal law. A rare instance of a plea of insanity succeeding in a criminal trial for causing injury with intent was in 1991 when the accused had been sleepwalking at the time of his violent assault upon a friend (see p. 179).

As regards civil rights and liabilities, insanity has a very restricted operation. A marriage contracted by a person so insane at the time as not to appreciate the nature of the obligations of the married state may be set aside at the suit of either party. The marriage of a person who has been judicially declared insane is totally void, and the same is said to be true of any disposition of property made by such a person. In general, however, the contract of a mentally disordered person is fully binding on him unless the other party was aware that he was so insane as not to understand the nature of the transaction. If these conditions are satisfied, the party suffering from mental disorders, on recovering his sanity, or those entitled to act on his behalf, may repudiate or confirm and enforce the contract. A person who is mentally disordered appears to be liable for wrongs, unless his disorder excludes some specific state of mind which forms an essential part of the wrong.

Drunkenness due to one's own fault is in itself no defence to a criminal charge; and this is probably true also of drunkenness not due to one's own fault—though no doubt the fact that it was not due to one's own fault would be a ground for mitigation of punishment. In all cases drunkenness may be material as showing that the accused had not the intention which forms part of the essence of the crime charged. Mental disease caused by drunkenness is in criminal law treated as on the same footing with insanity. In the matter of contract, drunkenness is regarded as having the same effect as insanity.

9. *The Crown and its servants*

The Queen, in her private capacity, is incapable of incurring liability, and no proceedings by way of action or prosecution can be taken against her. Government Departments can, however, under the Crown Proceedings Act 1947, be sued (*a*) for the recovery of property, (*b*) for breach of an ordinary commercial contract, but not for that of a contract of service, a contract dependent upon a future grant of money by Parliament, nor, it seems, one in which the Crown purports to fetter its own future executive action, or (*c*) for a tort. Servants of the Crown, from the highest executive, administrative, or military officers downwards, enjoy no general immunity for their public acts from either civil or criminal proceedings; and the command of a superior, even the command of the Queen, is no defence to any such proceedings. It is, of course, true that such officers in many cases have powers which enable them to do lawfully what a private person might not do, but the question whether their acts are justified by their powers must be decided in proceedings before the ordinary courts. A servant of the Crown is not himself liable for contracts made by him on behalf of the Crown, nor is he liable as a principal for the acts or defaults of his subordinates unless expressly authorized or subsequently ratified by him.

Judges enjoy an almost complete immunity in respect of acts—even corrupt and malicious acts, happily rare in our history—done by them in their judicial capacity. A judge of an inferior court, in order to entitle himself to this immunity, must, however, show that in reality, or at any rate upon the facts disclosed to him, he had jurisdiction in the matter in question.

Foreign sovereigns and the ambassadors of foreign states are immune from the jurisdiction of the English courts unless they voluntarily submit themselves to it, but the actual extent of the immunity is not free from doubt.

10. *Nationality and domicile*

All aliens, i.e. those who are not British citizens, used to be excluded from public office and public functions such as the parliamentary franchise. They had no enforceable right to enter British territory, and in some cases the Government was authorized by statute to exclude and even expel them from the United Kingdom. Some provisions of the criminal law applied only to British citizens, and certain other disabilities have been imposed by statute, especially on former enemy aliens. But in general the position of an alien in private law does not differ substantially from that of a British citizen, and the rule forbidding an alien to hold English land was abrogated in 1870. Most strikingly, the citizens of all countries within the European Union are now entitled to equal rights in all member countries, and so a citizen of, e.g., France or Denmark resident in the United Kingdom is entitled to vote in British parliamentary elections.

A radical change in the law relating to British nationality was effected by the British Nationality Act 1948. This reflected the conception of common citizenship between the various parts of the British Commonwealth. The essence of the scheme was that British nationality in the United Kingdom was achieved through citizenship of the United Kingdom and Colonies. This citizenship was attained (*a*) by birth in the United Kingdom, (*b*) by descent, (*c*) by registration, (*d*) by naturalization, or (*e*) by incorporation of territory. However, the weight of immigration to the United Kingdom of men and women from other Commonwealth territories, whether dependent or independent, necessitated a further change in 1981. The British Nationality Act 1981, which currently governs this topic, is based upon the aim, seen in many other countries, of making a person's nationality or citizenship accord with the country with which he is most really connected. Under the Act, which now replaces that of 1948, British citizenship is restricted to those with close personal connections with the United Kingdom, the Channel Islands or the Isle of Man. A child born in the United Kingdom will be a British citizen if the father or mother is a British citizen or settled in the United Kingdom in the sense of being entitled to stay indefinitely. Children born in the United Kingdom to students, visitors or illegal immigrants no longer automatically acquire British citizenship at birth, but they will still be able to register as British citizens if either parent later becomes a citizen or settles in the United Kingdom, or if the child has spent the first ten years of its life in the country. A child born abroad will be a British citizen by descent if either the father or mother was born or adopted in the United Kingdom or acquired citizenship by registration or naturalization. There are provisions for registration as British citizens of other children who do not automatically gain British citizenship by descent provided that there is some parental or grandparental link with the United Kingdom. There is also provision for the gaining of citizenship by naturalization by the Home Secretary.

An alien woman does not, as formerly, assume British citizenship automatically on marriage to a British citizen. Conversely, a woman who is a British citizen does not automatically lose her British citizenship on marriage with an alien. Loss of citizenship may be brought about in three ways, (*a*) naturalization in a foreign country, (*b*) in case of double citizenship, declaration of renunciation of British citizenship, (*c*) revocation of a certificate of naturalization.

More important for most purposes of private law than citizenship is domicile. The question, for instance, whether the goods of a person who dies intestate ought to be divided among his relations according to the rules of English or of some foreign law, will be decided by an English court, not according to the citizenship, but according to the domicile of the deceased at the time of his death. A person's domicile is the country which is in fact or in the eye of the law his permanent home for the time being. Seeing that our law refuses to contemplate the possibility of any person either being without a domicile or having more than one domicile, the rules on this subject are not only intricate but highly artificial. In 1987 the Law Commission recommended some radical change and simplification, but this has not yet been adopted. For the present we may note that every person is considered to start life with a 'domicile or origin', which will be, as a rule, the domicile of his father at the time of his birth; and that this domicile of origin continues until it is shown that some other domicile has been acquired, and is restored whenever an acquired domicile is lost without the acquisition of another. Formerly the domicile of a wife was necessarily the same as that of her husband, but under the Domicile and Matrimonial Proceedings Act 1973 the wife's dependent domicile was abolished: now her domicile is determined according to the same rules as for a single person. The substitution of citizenship for domicile in cases like that mentioned, after the manner of the law of some foreign countries, even if desirable on general grounds, would not solve the questions which arise when the laws of different parts of the same national territory, e.g. of England and Scotland, or of two states of the United States of America, come into competition. It is obvious that a pretty problem arises when the test of domicile refers the English courts to the law of a country which applies the test of citizenship and it happens that the citizenship of the person in question was British.

11. *Corporations*

Bodies or groups of human beings may have legally recognized rights and duties, which cannot be treated as the rights and duties of the members. Such bodies are known as corporations, or (to distinguish them from the corporations sole, to be mentioned later) corporations aggregate. The marks of a corporation are: (*a*) perpetual succession, i.e. the death or withdrawal of members, or the addition of new members from time to time, does not impair the continuity and identity of the body: 'in like manner', as Blackstone says, 'the river Thames is still the same river, though the parts which comprise it are changing every instant'; (*b*) the use of a common seal as evidence of at least the more formal acts of the corporation; and (*c*) the capacity to sue and be sued by its corporate name. The legal recognition of corporate character may be obtained either by a charter from the Crown, as in the case of most of our older corporations, like the Hudson's Bay Company, some universities and their colleges, as well as of some more recent ones; or directly by means of an incorporating Act of Parliament, as in the case of certain public utilities; or indirectly through an Act of Parliament like the Companies Act 1948 (which has been amended by several later Acts of the same name, and consolidated by the Companies Act 1985), which offers corporate character to any number of persons (usually not less than seven) associated for a lawful object, who are willing to comply with the statutory requirements as to registration and otherwise.

As a being capable of having legal rights and liabilities, a corporation is a person in the eye of the law. So far as English lawyers have theorized about the nature of corporate personality at all, they at one time for the most part accepted the doctrine of the Canon Law, that such personality is a mere fiction of the law with no basis in fact. But this doctrine has been largely supplanted by a later doctrine that such personality is real, and is analogous to the personality of individuals. It is impossible here to enter into the details of this controversy, but it may be noticed that

(1) the 'fiction theory' must remain unsatisfactory unless it can explain what are the real facts in terms of individual rights and duties which underlie the fiction, and this it seems

unable to do. It does not seem possible to explain away the legal rights and duties of a body as being merely the rights and duties of the individuals composing it; and

(2) the notion of a corporate personality is not confined to law. We habitually think of the actions of nations and of societies as distinct from the actions of the individuals composing them, and we attribute moral qualities to such actions, and moral rights and duties to nations and societies.

In fact it is impossible to deny the reality of the life and personality of many various groups and societies. It is because the State has recognized this fact that the law has insisted that, for a legal life and personality, these groups and societies must get the authority of the State, and submit to its conditions. The reason for this insistence is obvious. As Burke said, 'Liberty when men act in bodies is power.' The State can never be indifferent to the creation of a power or powers which may rival its own.

The legal capacity of corporations differs in some respects from that of individuals, partly from the nature of the case, partly as a consequence of the fact that their personality is an artificial one. It is obvious, for instance, that they cannot enter into family relations. Their amenability to the criminal law can never be the same as that of natural persons, though this has been increased by the powers conferred on judges and magistrates, by the Criminal Justice Act 1948, to impose a fine instead of imprisonment. On the other hand, a corporation can own property; it can acquire rights and make itself liable under a contract; it can be a trustee; it can incur civil liability for wrongful acts, and even for those which involve a definite state of mind like fraud or malice.

For the making of contracts by a corporation the Common Law required a document under the corporation's common seal, except in matters of trifling importance or daily necessary occurrence. Even apart from such exceptions, however, a contract not made in the required form, but completely performed on one side, might be enforced. The Common Law rule was partly destroyed by the Companies Acts, and, under the Corporate Bodies' Contracts Act 1960, contracts can now be made on behalf of all corporations in the same way as between private persons. The Companies Act 1989 goes still further by enabling corporations to execute almost all documents merely by signature.

Under the doctrine of *ultra vires*, there was a limit in point of substance on the transactions into which a corporation may enter. A Common Law corporation (i.e. one created by Charter from the Crown) is, it is true, presumed to have the contractual capacity of an individual. Prima facie such a corporation has the power to do with its property all such acts as an ordinary person can do, and to bind itself to such contracts as an ordinary person can bind himself to. Even if the Charter should contain restrictions on its freedom of action, acts transgressing such restrictions are probably not void, though they may be a ground for revoking the Charter. But a corporation created by or in pursuance of an Act of Parliament was subject to the rule that it had only such powers as were expressly conferred, or were necessarily or reasonably incident to the fulfilment of the purposes for which it was established. Acts done in excess of such powers were legally void, and could if necessary be restrained by the courts. One of the alterations effected in English law by the European Communities Act 1972 was that a person acting in good faith will not be prejudiced by any *ultra vires* transactions of a company, provided that the transaction was authorized by the company's directors. Eventually the Companies Act 1989 abolished the *ultra vires* rule altogether in company law. Now the acts of a company cannot generally be challenged simply because they are not permitted by the company's Memorandum and Articles of Association. Persons dealing with a company in good faith are protected against any limitation under the company's constitution on the power of the board of directors to bind the company or authorize others to do so.

Furthermore, a company formed under the Companies Act has a considerable power of altering the objects stated in the Memorandum and Articles of Association which are signed by its first members at the formation of the company, subject to the power of the holders of 15 per cent of its shares or debentures to apply to the court to cancel an alteration. This power may serve a number of purposes. It may prevent extraordinary powers, like that of compulsorily acquiring land, from being abused for unauthorized purposes; it may prevent a corporation, constituted for purposes of public utility, from endangering those purposes by engaging in other activities; it may protect the creditors of a company from the dissipation of the company's capital, to which alone, in the case of a limited company, they can look for payment, and the members from seeing their contributions applied to purposes for which they did not bargain. The Companies Act 1967, now consolidated in the Act of 1985, and added to by the Act of 1989, considerably strengthens the controls over the auditing of company accounts and the form of directors' reports. Among the matters which now have to be disclosed are directors' share dealings in their companies, and the amount of any contributions to political causes. Provisions designed to make it unlawful for companies to disclose to third parties information about a person's financial or personal affairs without his consent are contained in the Data Protection Act 1984 and the Criminal Justice and Public Order Act 1994.

In addition to corporations aggregate, English law attributes a continuous legal personality under the name of 'corporations sole' to the Queen, and to the successive holders of certain offices, especially the holders of ecclesiastical offices, such as bishops, and rectors and vicars of parishes. The conception, however, as applied to the Queen, and to these ecclesiastical persons, has not, for historical reasons, produced satisfactory results, and the Church of England has set up a Commission which is thought likely to recommend abolition of the 'parson's freehold'. The General Synod of the Church of England has already decided in 1994 to implement the recommendation by another Commission to abolish the similar security of tenure enjoyed by the deans and canons of cathedrals. But it is a useful conception; and it has been applied by statute to some public officers, such as certain Ministers and the Official Solicitor.

12. *Societies and institutions*

There are no prohibitions against the formation of associations or societies for any lawful object—religious, social, political, philanthropic, or the like. The law does not, however, regard such societies (unless formally incorporated) as having any corporate personality; it sees only individuals, owning property, it may be, in common, with rights and duties towards each other flowing from the contract, or rather series of contracts, to be found in the society's rules; for on every change in the membership a new contract must be implied. Such contract or contracts may be varied if, and only if, the rules so provide, by a majority of the members or by a specified majority. The common property, if it is more than mere cash in hand or at the bank, will be vested in trustees who must deal with it in accordance with the rules or with any trust expressly declared, and it can be made liable for obligations incurred by, or on behalf of, the society. But no liability for tort can be enforced against a Trade Union for acts done in contemplation or furtherance of a specific trade dispute (within strict limits), and possibly not against other unincorporated societies. Where the objects of the society are charitable in the legal sense, which includes the relief of poverty, the advancement of education or religion, and other purposes beneficial to the community, formalities prescribed by older statutes have been abolished by the Charities Act 1960, now consolidated in the Charities Act 1993, which, however, provides for compulsory registration of all charities not especially exempted. If the objects of the society are not charitable, the rule against perpetuities (see p. 46), from which charities, provided that they are to begin within the perpetuity period, are exempt, will make void any gift of property by way of permanent endowment, whether made by will or otherwise; but there is nothing to prevent gifts or bequests from being made to a non-charitable society in such terms that it can, at any time, dispose of the capital at its pleasure. The rules of a society and the trusts which bind its property will, in many cases, fetter its freedom of action and the application of its property; and the

Charities Act 1992, now consolidated in the 1993 Act, extends powers to supervise and investigate charities, and to regulate their accounting and reporting procedures. In the case of some unincorporated societies, such as registered Trade Unions and Friendly Societies, which have received a peculiar status by statute, the rule of *ultra vires* has been held directly applicable. But, subject to considerable restrictions on the furtherance of political objects, a Trade Union is empowered by statute since 1913 to devote its funds to any lawful objects authorized by its rules for the time being.

Some systems of law recognize as legal persons, not only corporations, but institutions, such as hospitals or places of education; but this conception is unknown to our law. We either treat as a corporation a group of persons—usually the governing body of the institution, though it may include individuals who are beneficiaries and have no share in the government (for instance, the scholars of a college)—or else the property of the institution must be vested in a number of individual trustees, who are bound to apply and deal with it for the purposes of the institution.

13. *Agency and partnership*

Agency may be regarded as an extension of legal personality. Not only in law, but in ordinary life, we look upon an act done by one man in pursuance of another's orders as done by the person who gives the order. Moreover, there seems to be nothing artificial in principle in holding the acts of an employee done in the course of his employment as equivalent to the acts of the employer. These principles are, however, applied in different degrees in the respective spheres of Criminal and Civil Law.

A man is not punishable for a serious crime committed by another unless he has actually instigated the commission of a crime, and then he will be punishable though the crime committed may differ in some degree from that which he instigated. It may be noted that in Criminal Law anyone who aids, counsels, or procures the commission of an offence is liable to be tried and punished in the same way as if he were a principal offender. But in the case of minor offences, and especially statutory offences, which are anti-social rather than immoral, a man may be punished even for the unauthorized act or default of one in his employment.

In the case of wrongful acts, which involve civil liability apart from breach of contract or trust, a distinction is drawn between a servant and an independent contractor. A servant is one over whom the employer reserves the control and direction of the mode in which the work is to be done. The master is liable for wrongful acts and defaults of his servant—though they may be unauthorized or even forbidden by him—so long as they are done within the scope of the employment. An omnibus company was held liable for the act of one of its drivers, who overturned a rival omnibus while racing with it and obstructing it, although directions had been issued to the driver forbidding such conduct. The independent contractor is one who has agreed to do a piece of work, but is to be left free to choose his own method of doing it. In such cases the employer is not liable in general for any wrong which consists in the improper carrying out of such work, though he will, of course, be liable if unlawful acts are done which he has actually authorized.

Contracts made by any agent in pursuance of the principal's instructions are binding on, and operate for the benefit of, the latter. Further, the employment of an agent may be such as to give him an authority to contract on behalf of his principal generally with regard to a wider or narrower class of affairs; and as between the principal and third parties such authority cannot be limited by restrictions imposed by the principal, but not known to third parties.

The fact that a person is acting under the instructions or on behalf of another is no defence to civil or criminal proceedings brought against the agent for tort or crime. On the other hand, an agent acquires no rights under contracts made by him on behalf of his principal; and where the existence of the principal is known to those contracting with the agent, the latter, as a rule, incurs no liability for such contracts. Where the principal's existence is undisclosed, the other contracting party, on discovering it, has an option whether he will hold agent or principal liable.

When a person purports to act on behalf of another, but without his authority, the latter may subsequently ratify the act of the former, and thereby draw to himself both the benefit of, and the liability for, the act. But if there is no such ratification, the agent will be liable to those who contract on the faith of the authority which he professes to have.

No special form is necessary for the appointment of an agent, except that an agent who is to execute documents under seal in the name of his principal must be appointed by a 'power of attorney', which is itself a document under seal. Revocation by the principal, his death, and in some cases his insanity, put an end to the agent's authority, though in general a revocation will be inoperative as against those to whom the principal has held out the agent as having authority, and who have no notice of the revocation. Moreover, modern legislation has made possible (within limits) the creation of an irrevocable power of attorney, so that even knowledge of the principal's death or insanity will not affect the validity of acts done under it.

An agent must not, without his principal's knowledge and consent, receive any reward or commission from those with whom he deals on his principal's behalf, or derive any profit from transactions entered into on the principal's behalf beyond the remuneration agreed upon. Both civil and criminal liability are incurred by the corrupt giving or receiving of such commission.

In partnership, which is 'the relation which subsists between persons carrying on a business in common with a view of profit', every partner is an agent of the firm and of the other partners for the purpose of the business of the partnership. A firm is not in England a legal personality distinct from its members, though in Scotland a firm is a legal person distinct from the partners of whom it is composed (Partnership Act 1890, s. 4(2)). In an ordinary partnership each of the partners is liable without limit for all the debts and obligations of the firm. The severity of this rule has been the more acutely felt because the existence of a partnership, which needs no special form for its creation, has often been inferred—less often, it is true, in recent years than formerly—from the fact of the receipt by a person of a share of the profits of a business. Since 1907 the law has permitted the formation of 'limited partnerships', which must be registered and must consist of at least one general partner, who is liable without limit, and of one or more limited partners, each of whom is not liable beyond the amount contributed by him on entering into the partnership. A limited partner is forbidden, on pain of rendering his liability unlimited, to take any part in the management of the business, and has no power to bind the firm. But limited partnerships are rare, private companies, which were sanctioned the next year by the Companies Act 1908, having proved more popular. No partnership, whether limited or unlimited, may consist of more than twenty persons.

14. *Enemy status*

In time of war, persons for the time being residing or doing business in an enemy country, whatever their nationality or domicile, are disabled from suing in the English Courts; but if sued here they will so far as possible be given an opportunity of defending themselves. Every communication for commercial or other purposes, by those in this country, with such persons or bodies is a criminal offence ('trading with the enemy'), unless licensed by the Crown. Any contract or transaction, the formation or execution of which involves such communication, is (or, if made before the war, becomes) void.

5 Property

1. *The conception of property*

There is perhaps nothing more difficult than to give a precise and consistent meaning to the word 'property'. The word 'estate' is often used to denote the whole of a man's proprietary rights, more especially after his death. This sense of the word 'estate' must not be confused with the special meaning which it has in regard to interests in land (see p. 88). When we speak of a man of property, we may perhaps think in one of two ways. First, we may think of the traditional or even old-fashioned type of man with tangible material things which belong to him—land and houses, horses and cattle, furniture and jewellery and pictures— things which he may use or destroy (so far as that is physically possible); from which he may exclude others; which he may sell or give away or bequeath; which, if he has made no disposition of them, will pass on his death to persons related to him. Alternatively we may think of the more modern figure of a man whose wealth lies in his investments in stocks and shares. Whichever type of man we think of, we may find it difficult to say whether by 'property' we mean the things themselves or the aggregate of rights which are exercised over them. To confine the word to either sense would hardly be possible without pedantry; though on the one hand we may agree that a thing which has no owner—a rare event in a civilized country, except in the case of a few things, like wild animals at large—is not property, and on the other we may often avoid confusion by using the word 'ownership' for the most extensive right which a man can have over material things. But, further, we shall find that our conception of property relates to many things which are not tangible or material. Our man of property may be an author or a patentee, and we shall hardly be able to say that his copyright or patentright is not part of his property, or even to avoid speaking of his ownership of the copyright or patent. He will have debtors: his bank is a debtor to him for the amount standing to his credit; his investments of money are claims to receive payment from the State or from corporations or individuals. Such debts and claims are not rights over any specific tangible objects; they are mere rights against the State or the corporation or the person liable to pay. Yet these rights are transferable, and will pass on his death to his representatives. We cannot exclude them from our notion of property or deny that in a sense, at any rate, he is the owner of them. On the other hand his 'property' clearly does not include all his rights. To say nothing of his general right of liberty or reputation, his rights as a husband or a parent are not proprietary rights, nor is his right to recover damages for personal injury or defamation; but we may include among proprietary rights the right to recover damages though unliquidated (i.e. of uncertain amount until settled by a judge or jury) for breach of contract, or probably even for injury to his property. Generally speaking we shall include under the notion of a man's property in its widest sense all rights which are capable of being transferred to others, of being made available for payment of his debts, or of passing to his representatives on his death.

2. *Ownership and possession*

Turning to rights over tangible things, we must notice the distinction between ownership and possession. The owner of a thing is the person who has, in the fullest degree, those rights of use and enjoyment, of destruction, and of disposition, which have been mentioned above—subject of course to the general rules of law which protect the rights of others, to certain limited rights which he or his predecessors may have created in favour of others, and in the case of land to rules imposed by statute under which local and other authorities may purchase property compulsorily. The owner of a firearm is none the less owner because the law prohibits him from discharging it in a public highway; the owner of a field does not cease to be owner because the public or a neighbour has the right to use a footpath across it. Nor is ownership infringed by the Access to Neighbouring Land Act 1992, which allows a person a right of access on to neighbouring land in order to carry out certain types of repair and maintenance work on his own land.

The essence of ownership, then, is that it is a right or an aggregate of rights. Possession, on the other hand, is primarily a matter of fact. If the owner of a watch is robbed of it by a thief, the owner's rights as rights remain intact; the thief acquires no right to the watch as against the owner. (An ancient exception called 'sale in market overt', whereby buyers of stolen goods in certain old street markets gained good title to them if they acted in good faith, was abolished by the Sale of Goods (Amendment) Act 1994.) But the owner's possession, and with it his actual power to exercise his rights, is for the time being gone; he must recover the watch—as he may even lawfully do by his own act—before he can be said to be again in possession of it. So too the owner of land may be out of possession, and another without right may be in possession. In this case the forcible retaking of possession is prohibited under penalties by statute; but the retaking, though punishable, is none the less effective to restore the possession.

The cases of the thief and the squatter have been taken as the clearest instances of possession acquired without any right whatever. But possession may be lawfully acquired, and yet be unaccompanied by ownership. An owner who delivers a car or a bicycle by way of loan or hire to another parts with the possession to him, but does not cease to be owner. The same is true of one who delivers articles to another in order that the latter may bestow his labour upon them. Such voluntary transfers of possession are called bailment, and the person who so acquires possession is a bailee of the goods. In none of these cases do we think of the owner as having parted with the right of ownership, though it may be that the contract between the parties creates rights in favour of the bailee which the owner cannot use his right of ownership to override.

If we try to analyse the conception of possession, we find two elements. In the first place it involves some actual power of control over the thing possessed. In the second place it involves some intention to maintain that control on the part of the possessor. The nature and extent of the control and intention necessary to constitute possession will vary with the circumstances, and particularly with the character of the thing of which the possession is in question. Possession of a house, for instance, will be evidenced by acts different from those which would suffice for possession of a strip of waste land. The occupier of a private house (but not the owner of a house who had never entered into possession of it) would probably be considered to be in possession of anything placed or left in it—at any rate unless it was concealed—while the occupier of a shop has been held not to be in possession of a thing dropped in a part of the shop to which the public had access. By a somewhat artificial rule, a servant who receives a thing from his master for the master's use is deemed not to be in possession of it, though the contrary is true where he receives it from a stranger for the master's use.

So far we have thought of ownership and possession as sharply distinguished—the one a matter of right, the other of fact. Nevertheless possession is a fact which has an enormous legal significance, a fact to which legal rights are attached. In the first place actual possession is evidence of ownership, and, except in cases where ownership is based on a system of public registration, it is hard to see how any ownership can be proved, otherwise than by going back to some prior possession. If A claims the ownership of land by reason of B's bequest or sale to him, this only raises the question, On what is B's ownership based? and ultimately we shall have to rest content with saying that the root of A's title is the possession of some predecessor, X. Such evidence, however, is not conclusive. The presumption of ownership which follows from A's or X's possession may, for instance, be rebutted by a rival claimant, Y, who can show that he or his predecessor was in possession, and that A or X wrongfully dispossessed him.

In the second place possession is not merely evidence of ownership, but (subject to the rights of the owner) is itself and for its own sake entitled to legal protection. If A has been disturbed in his possession by a trespass committed by B, or even if B has deprived A of possession, A's claim to legal protection or redress against B cannot be met by B's plea that C and not A is the true owner. The finder of goods is entitled—except only against one who can show himself to be the owner—to legal protection against all the world. Nor is this right of the possessor based on any responsibility on his part to the owner. The Postmaster-General (later the Minister of Posts and Telecommunications) was held entitled to recover damages for the loss of the mails destroyed by the fault of a colliding ship, though he was not the owner and disclaimed all responsibility to the owners for the loss. This right to redress which the law confers on the possessor is independent of, and at least as old as, if not older than, the legal protection given to the owner. The possessor's right is even spoken of as a 'special property', in contradistinction to the 'general property' of the owner. It is a right which he may transfer, and which on his death will pass under his will or according to the rules of intestacy.

Lastly, we may notice that even a wrongful possession, if continued for a certain length of time, matures into what may be, for practical purposes, indistinguishable from ownership. A wrongful possession of land for twelve years, or of goods for six years, destroys not only the former owner's right to recover the land or goods by action, but also his title; and so the possessor has the best of titles known to the law—a possession which no one can dispute.

3. *Real property and personal property*

Between the ownership of land and of goods every system of law must needs draw distinctions, which are founded on the nature of the subject-matter. But the distinctions drawn by English law were, till the passing of the Property Acts, which came into force on 1 January 1926, founded, not so much on the nature of the subject-matter, as upon the historical accidents in the development of the English law of property.[1] Property was divided into the two categories of real property and personal property; and personal property was divided into two categories of chattels real and chattels personal.

Real property included most of the interests in land recognized by the law, and other rights, such as easements and profits (see p. 92), annexed to the land. This property was called 'real' because, from the first, it was recoverable specifically by a real action. In fact anything thus recoverable was real property. Property thus recoverable developed a set of legal characteristics which caused it to differ considerably from property which was recoverable only by a personal action; and so, though the real actions have long been abolished, and for a still longer time disused, the differences between real and personal property survived.

Not all the interests in land known to the law were included in the category of real property. Interests in land for a term of years (leaseholds) were originally regarded, not as interests in the land, but as contractual rights. The lessee was protected, not by a real action, but by a personal action against his lessor, in which he could recover, not the land itself, but only damages for the breach of his landlord's contract to allow him the use of the land. Hence his interest is personal property, and is classed as a chattel, though, by reason of its close relation to real property, it is distinguished as a chattel real. Leaseholders long since obtained remedies for the specific recovery of their land: and those remedies were in fact far superior to the old real actions. But because these interests in land were protected by personal and not by the real actions they developed a set of legal characteristics which caused them to differ from the interests classed as real property. Notable differences were to be found in the rules as to succession on intestacy and in the variety of estates and interests which could be created in these two kinds of property.

All property other than real property and chattels real is classed as chattels personal. Chattels personal consist either of tangible goods or of intangible rights such as patents, or stocks and shares. They differ from real property in two main respects. First, chattels personal can be owned, while real property is held mediately or immediately of the Queen. Secondly, until 1926, at law (as opposed to equity) no limited interests in chattels personal could be created—the notion of estates had no application to chattels personal till the Law of Property Act 1925 made it possible to create an entailed interest in them. In this respect equity differed from the common law. We shall see that it was always possible to settle chattels personal upon trusts for various persons with limited interests (see pp. 97–9, 114–18).

4. *Tenure*

In the medieval period it was a very significant legal commonplace that full ownership of land was possible for no person save the King. Those commonly called landowners were regarded as 'holding' their land, by various forms of 'tenure', of the King. Of these the most honourable, but at the same time the most burdensome, was tenure by knight service, which involved many irksome 'incidents' (see Chapter 2, note 1). The incidents of socage tenure consisted of fixed and nominal agricultural services. By the Statute of Tenures 1660 all free tenures (with insignificant exceptions) were converted into socage.[2] Though 1660 marked the end of feudalism in its political aspect, in the sphere of private law it continued to cause many difficulties, which were not removed until 1925. One practical mark of its survival was the doctrine of escheat. If a socage tenant died without heirs and intestate, his land escheated, i.e. went back to the lord of whom it was held, who in practically all cases had come to be the King. A statute called *Quia Emptores* (1290) had enacted that whenever a tenant alienated his land for an estate in fee simple the alienee should hold, not of the alienor, but of the alienor's lord. The long-term result of this statute was that practically all land held by free tenure had come to be held of the King. Escheat was swept away, together with the old law of intestate succession, by the new scheme introduced by the Administration of Estates Act 1925.

5. *Estates in possession*

The different types of tenure marked out the leading characteristics of the different forms of land holding known to the law; but they told us nothing of the nature and incidents of the various interests which those who held by these tenures might have in the land. It is this question of the nature and incidents of these interests which we must now consider.

The word used by English law to denote the tenant's interest in the land is the word 'estate'. An estate is a portion of the ownership of the land, more or less limited in time. This limitation in time is most clearly seen in the case of a life estate, whether it be an estate held for the life of the tenant, or what is called an estate *pur autre vie*, one held for the life or lives of some other person or persons. The holder of such an estate in land is, like an owner, entitled to the possession, use, and enjoyment of the land, and he can dispose of his interest; but at the death of the person by whose life the extent of his estate is measured the estate comes to an end, and nothing passes from the holder. Even the holder's enjoyment is restricted (unless he be declared 'unimpeachable for waste') by consideration for the rights of those who have subsequent estates in the land. He must not diminish the capital value of the land by the commission of acts called 'waste', such as cutting timber or opening mines.

At the other end of the scale we have the estate in fee simple. Such an estate is practically equivalent to ownership. It confers full rights of possession and enjoyment (unrestricted by any rules as to waste) and full rights of disposition whether during the tenant's lifetime or by his will. If he dies intestate, the land will pass to his relations entitled in that event (see pp. 126–8 for the modern law on this subject). Only in the event of his death intestate, and without relations so entitled, will the estate come to an end and the land pass to the Crown. The limit in time is here practically non-existent.

Intermediate between the life estate and the estate in fee simple is the estate tail. The tenant in tail has full rights of possession and enjoyment without regard to waste. Nor does the estate come to an end with the tenant's death: it passes to his heirs, but only to a limited class of heirs, 'the heirs of his body', that is, his descendants. (For the rules of inheritance for ascertaining the heir, see pp. 125–8.) The line of descent may be further restricted by making the estate an estate in tail-male, i.e. one descendible only to males and only in the male line, or conceivably (though in practice this appears never to be done) in tail-female descendible only to and through females. There is even an estate known as an estate in 'special tail', inheritable only by the issue of the tenant by a certain wife or husband. In the latter case, if the wife or husband dies without issue the tenant is said to be tenant in tail, 'after possibility of issue extinct', and his rights are substantially no greater than those of a tenant for life. Before 1926 a tenant in tail had no power to dispose of his estate by will; but a tenant in tail in possession could in his lifetime, and still can, bar the entail by a deed, i.e. he can turn it into a fee simple estate. If his estate is not in possession, e.g. if it is limited to A for life and then to B in tail, A is the 'Protector of the settlement', and B cannot bar the entail without A's consent.

We shall see that, since 1 January 1926, the only one of these estates which survives as a legal estate is the estate in fee simple. The others exist only as equitable interests. Their incidents are similar to the incidents of the old legal estates, though certain important changes have been introduced (see p. 97–9).

6. *Estates* in futuro

Before 1 January 1926 there were three main varieties of legal estates *in futuro*.

(1) *Reversions and remainders.* An estate for life was less than an estate tail, and both were smaller than a fee simple. Suppose

now that a tenant in fee simple granted the land to another to hold for life or in tail. If he did nothing more he would still retain his fee simple, but he would have deprived himself of the right to present possession and enjoyment of the land; his estate would become a future estate, which would again become a present estate, an 'estate in possession', only when the smaller estate, the 'particular estate' which had been carved out of it, came to an end. For the time being, what was left to him was called a reversion. Further, he might by the same instrument grant a present estate, say for life, to A, followed by an estate for life or in tail to B, and, if he wished, as many further particular estates (for life or in tail) to other persons successively as he pleased, ending up, if he thought fit, with an estate in fee simple to some person named. Each of these future estates was called a remainder. No reversion or remainder, however, could be placed after a fee simple. Each of these future estates, though it gave no present right to possession or enjoyment, was treated as something already in existence, which could be disposed of and would descend (so far as it is inheritable) just like a present estate. If, for instance, A was tenant for life and B tenant in fee simple in reversion or remainder, B's death before A's would not destroy the estate in fee simple, but B's heir, or the person to whom B had conveyed it by deed, or left it by will, was entitled to come in on A's death. So again, if A was tenant in tail, and B tenant in fee simple in reversion, the failure of A's issue at his death, or at any later time, would vest the fee simple in possession in whatever person then represented B. In such cases ownership, we may say, was cut up into lengths called estates. None of the holders of an estate, except the tenant in fee simple when in possession, was fully owner, but each as he came into possession was a 'limited' owner.

(2) *Shifting and springing uses.* We have seen that, if A held land to the use of B, the Statute of Uses turned B's equitable estate into a legal estate (see p. 25). Now it was possible for a settlor who conveyed land to A to direct him to hold to the use of B; and then to direct that, on the happening of an event, e.g.

B's marriage, B's use should shift to C. This use in favour of C was a shifting use. Or the settlor could direct that in a certain event a new use should spring up in D's favour. This use in favour of D was a springing use. When the use in favour of C or D arose, C or D's uses were turned into legal estates by the Statute of Uses.

(3) *Executory devises.* The Statute of Wills 1540 gave testators power to create future legal estates by their wills. These estates were known as executory devises.

We shall see that since 1 January 1926 none of these future legal estates can be created, but that similar results can be effected by the creation of future equitable interests through the medium of a trust.

7. *Co-ownership*

Co-ownership entitles two or more persons concurrently to the possession and enjoyment of the same land. Before 1 January 1926 it could take three forms: coparcenary, or tenancy in common, or joint tenancy. Coparcenary existed if a person died intestate leaving two or more females as his heirs. They took the land as coparceners. When two or more persons took as tenants in common, the share of each was treated as a separate item of property which could not only be transferred by him in his lifetime, but which would pass on his death to his representatives. In the case of joint tenancy, on the other hand, the rights of each (except the last survivor) are extinguished by his death so as to increase the interest of the survivor or survivors. A joint tenant might, however, transfer his interest in his lifetime (though not by will); and such a transfer would, before 1 January 1926, have had the effect of making the transferee a tenant in common with the other or others, though the others continued as between themselves to be joint tenants. Any one of a number of co-owners was entitled to have the property 'partitioned', i.e. divided, or at any rate to have the property sold and his share paid out to him. Where a number of trustees are appointed they are always made joint tenants, in order that, on the death of one, the whole property may be vested in the survivors; but in other cases joint tenancy is inconvenient and rarely occurs. We shall see that since 1 January 1926 the only one of these three forms of co-ownership which exists as a legal estate is joint tenancy (see p. 98); but that both coparcenary and tenancy in common exist as equitable estates.

Both ownership in common and joint ownership may exist in the case of chattels personal as well as in the case of land.

8. *Other interests in land*

Besides the interests in land which are known as estates, and which, when they are present estates, give a right to possession of the land, English law, like other systems, recognizes rights of a more restricted kind. Among these we may notice *easements*, such as rights of way, rights of light, rights to take water or to discharge water over the land of another. A true easement must always be 'appurtenant' to a piece of land. An individual cannot, for instance, as such have a right of way over my land, but only as owner of some adjacent piece of land. Rights similar to easements may, however, exist in favour of the public, e.g. a public highway; or in favour of a limited class—e.g. the fishermen of a village may by custom have the right to dry their nets on a piece of land, the inhabitants of a village may have a right to use the village green for purposes of recreation. *Profits à prendre* are rights to take things of value (other than water) from land, such as the right of common pasture, or rights of fishery (commoners, it should be noticed, are not owners of the common). Such rights, though commonly appendant or appurtenant to land—there is little practical difference between the two phrases—are not necessarily so. They may exist in favour of individuals, and in some cases in favour of a limited class, but, with the exception of the public right of fishing in tidal water, they cannot exist in favour of the public at large.

The effect of long-continued possession of land in extinguishing adverse rights, and so converting the possession into what is indistinguishable from ownership, has already been referred to (see p. 85). Different in theory, but similar in effect, are the provisions of the Prescription Act 1832, under which rights to easements and *profits à prendre* may be established by reason of enjoyment for a period of not less than twenty years in the one case, and not less than thirty in the other. Special rules as to the acquisition of public rights of way by lapse of time have been made by the Rights of Way Act 1932.

A rentcharge is the right to receive an annual sum out of the income of land, usually in perpetuity, and to distrain if the payments are in arrear; the owner of the land is also personally liable to pay, and further remedies against the land have been given by statute. In some parts of the country it has been the practice to sell freehold land for building, and to take the price in the form of a perpetual rentcharge created by the purchaser; this practice took the place of the more common building lease. The Rentcharges Act 1977 prohibited the creation of further rentcharges, and provided also for the extinguishment of all existing rentcharges at the end of sixty years starting on 22 July 1977, or on the date the rentcharge first became payable, whichever is later. Alternatively a rentcharge may, under the 1977 Act, be bought out by a lump sum payment.

The right to take tithes, i.e. a share of the produce of the land in kind, originally vested only in ecclesiastical persons and bodies, was at the Reformation transferred in many cases to laymen, though tithes continued to form the most important kind of ecclesiastical endowment. Under the legislation of the nineteenth century tithes were commuted into tithe rentcharge, an annual sum varying with the price of corn. In 1936 tithe rentcharge was abolished. Tithe owners were compensated by the issue to them of redemption stock charged on the Consolidated Fund, and land charged with tithe was charged instead with redemption annuities payable to the Crown. Such redemption annuities were originally intended to be payable until 1996, but they were ended by the Finance Act 1977, and the final payments (of double the normal sum) were made on 1 October 1977. The rights of presentation to livings in the Church of

England, known as advowsons, which are often in the hands of laymen, are also regarded as interests in land. But the effect of a Measure of the Church Assembly of 1923 has been to render advowsons virtually inalienable, except in the case of a sale of land to which an advowson is appendant.

9. *Chattels real*

The most important class of chattels real are leasehold estates. A leasehold estate is measured by a fixed period of time; it is often called a term of years, though a tenancy for weeks or months is equally a leasehold. There is no superior limit; a term of 1,000 or 10,000 years (such terms actually occur) is still a leasehold. Nor does a term cease to be a leasehold because it is determinable by an event which may happen, or which is certain to happen, within the term—e.g. if A holds land for 99 years or for 999 years, 'if he shall so long live', he is still a leaseholder, though it is nearly or quite certain that he will not outlive the term. A freeholder may grant a lease of any duration, though unless he is a tenant in fee simple, or the lease is made under the powers given by the Settled Land Acts, the lease will fail when the lessor dies. A leaseholder (unless prohibited by his own lease) can himself grant a lease for any term less than that which he holds; a grant for an equal or greater term would be merely a transfer of his own interest.

Between the grantor of a leasehold and the tenant (lessor and lessee) there is a relation of tenure, and while the lease subsists the lessor has a reversion. The most important incident of the reversion is the lessor's right to the rent reserved by the lease, generally substantial and often equal to the full annual value of the property. This right he can enforce not only by action, but also by a form of self-help known as distress, the seizure of any goods, whether belonging to the tenant or to a stranger, which may be found on the premises. Originally this was merely a method of putting pressure upon the tenant, but the distrainer has had, since the end of the seventeenth century, a power to sell the goods and so pay himself, the surplus (if any) going to the owner. Legislation has largely restricted the right to distrain goods found upon the premises but not belonging to the tenant.

The rights and duties of the leasehold tenant are, as a rule, explicitly provided for by the terms of the lease, which will contain covenants such as those relating to payment of rent, repair, cultivation, and building, or forbidding the carrying on of certain trades. Such covenants, so far as they relate to the premises leased, are binding on and enforceable by assignees both of lessor and lessee. The lessor is usually further protected by a proviso allowing him to re-enter and put an end to the lease in the event of the tenant's failure to pay rent or observe the other covenants. A proviso for re-entry in the event of the tenant's assigning or underletting the premises without the lessor's consent was sometimes enforced in the most oppressive way; but, under the Landlord and Tenant Act 1927, a proviso that the consent is not to be unreasonably withheld is implied; and in this case, and in other cases, with one or two exceptions, the courts have power to give relief to the tenant. Moreover, in most cases, the right to re-enter cannot be exercised until the tenant has been given an opportunity of making good the breach of covenant. At the end of the lease the tenant must yield up the premises, together with all buildings, fixtures, trees, and plants thereon, including even what he has himself added; but to some extent this rule is relaxed in favour of trade and agricultural fixtures; and a right to remove tenants' fixtures may be given by the terms of the lease. Under the Agricultural Holdings Act 1948 tenants of agricultural land, and under the Landlord and Tenant Acts 1927 and 1954 other lessees, are entitled to claim compensation from their landlords for many improvements made by them, and also in some cases compensation for the disturbance by reason of notices to quit. Recent legislation has had some effect in keeping rents within reasonable bounds, and in providing security of tenure for tenants against landlords; and under the Landlord and Tenant Act 1987 many residential tenants now have a right of first refusal where the landlord proposes to dispose of his interest in the property.

A special form of leasehold is the tenancy from year to year, which continues until notice to put an end to it is given by either party. In ordinary cases the notice must be a six months' notice, ending with a completed year, but in the case of agricultural tenancies the Agricultural Holdings Act 1923 requires a full year's notice. Another variant is the shorthold tenancy, created by the Housing Act 1980, whereby the lessor and lessee agree to a fixed-term letting of a period not less than one and not more than five years certain, carrying with it automatic security of tenure for the period agreed.

Closely akin to leaseholds, and like them classed as personal interests in land, are tenancies at will and at sufferance. The former is a tenancy made by the agreement of the parties on the terms that either may put an end to it at any moment at the shortest notice; the latter arises where a tenant whose interest has expired continues in possession without the landlord either assenting or dissenting.

The Leasehold Reform Act 1967 for the first time introduced leasehold enfranchisement, whereby a lessee is entitled to compel his lessor to sell him the freehold upon payment of compensation on a scale fixed by the Act. By no means all leases came under these provisions. For a tenant to claim the benefits of the Act he had to show that his tenancy was of a house, that it was originally granted for more than twenty-one years, that the rent payable was less than two-thirds of its rateable value, and that the rateable value was itself not in excess of certain modest limits. A side effect of the Act has been that many owners of leasehold property no longer regard such investments as sound, as they have voluntarily negotiated the sale of freeholds even where the property concerned did not fall within the provisions of the 1967 Act. And the process has been carried further by the Leasehold Reform, Housing, and Urban Development Act 1993, which is based upon the condominium laws which operate successfully in the USA, Australia, New Zealand, and certain other countries. The Act gives tenants of flats the right either to enfranchise their blocks of flats collectively or to seek extensions of their existing leases individually. Similar qualifying conditions apply as for leaseholders of houses, but it is now provided that tenants may buy their homes on 'rent to mortgage' terms, i.e. a tenant may make an initial payment which can be financed by a mortgage, and will then repay the mortgage by regular sums equivalent to the current rent. The tenants of at least two-thirds of the total number of flats in the premises must be in favour of enfranchisement before the provisions of the Act apply, and there are a number of other detailed requirements before any opposition by the landlord can be overcome. The scheme works on the basis that each individual unit within a building may be owned freehold, and that the owners then belong to a 'common-hold association', consisting of the unit owners, which owns and manages any common parts of the building. Mutual rights and obligations flow from the 1993 Act. All in all, commonhold may be seen as a significant modern variation upon freehold tenure.

10. *The Property Acts*

The three main objects of these Acts[1] are,

(1) to get rid of the artificial distinctions which the historical development of the law had drawn between land and movable property—leaving only those distinctions which are due to the natural qualities of these two forms of property;

(2) to assimilate the law relating to chattels real and real property, and, so far as this is possible, the law relating to land and movable property; and

(3) to simplify and cheapen dealings in land. The principal changes in the law by which the framers of these Acts have sought to effect these objects can be summarized as follows:

(i) One of the leading differences between real and personal property was their devolution on intestacy. The Administration of Estates Act 1925 has, as we shall see, provided a uniform scheme of intestate succession for all kinds of property. Similarly, if a man died without heirs and intestate, the process by which the land devolved to the Crown was different. Real property escheated to the Crown: personal property devolved on the Crown as *bona vacantia*. Escheat has been abolished, and all property in such a case devolves on the Crown as *bona vacantia*.

(ii) The abolition of escheat has meant the abolition of the last of the practical consequences of free tenure. Tenure is now only important as between a lessor for a term of years and his lessee.

(iii) Great simplifications have been made in the law as to estates and interests in land, with the result that the law of property has been made very much more uniform.

(*a*) The Law of Property Act 1925 reduces the number of legal estates in the land to two—a fee simple absolute in possession, and a term of years absolute. The estate of the tenant from year to year is included in the term of years absolute; and the interests of a tenant at will and at sufferance are still recognized. The other estates exist, but as equitable, not as legal, interests.

(*b*) Estates tail, which formerly could only be created out of freeholds, can now, as equitable interests, be created out of any kind of property; they are known as 'entailed interests', and can be barred not only *inter vivos* by a deed, but also by a will, provided that the tenant in tail's interest is in possession, and provided that he specifically refers in his will to the entailed property or the instrument creating it.

(*c*) The Statute of Uses has been repealed; and future legal estates in real property cannot now be created. Such estates can now only be created as equitable interests by means of the machinery of a trust. This has always been the only way in which future interests in personal property can be created. The result is that future estates and interests in all kinds of property are now assimilated.

(*d*) Legal tenancy in common gave rise to great difficulties in the tracing of titles to land, because it was necessary to investigate separately the title of each tenant. It is therefore abolished as a legal estate. When formerly two or more persons would have taken as legal tenants in common, they take now as joint tenants on trust for the tenants in common; and no severance of this legal joint tenancy by alienation or otherwise is allowed. Owing to the changes made in the law of intestate succession (see pp. 125–8), coparcenary can exist only in the case of an entailed interest.

(*e*) For a long period real property was only liable to certain of the debts of its deceased owner: chattels real and personal were always liable to all the debts of a deceased person which survived his death. Even when real property was made liable to all these debts, it was made liable by a different process and in a different order from personal property. The Administration of Estates Act 1925 has provided a uniform method for the administration of all the property of a deceased person.

11. *Conveyances of land*

From a very early period the courts have been opposed to restrictions upon the free alienation of land. In the thirteenth century they got rid of old restrictions which fettered the freedom of alienation in the interest of lords or heirs. The Statute of *Quia Emptores* 1290 gave free power of alienation *inter vivos* to all tenants in fee simple; and the effect of the Statute of Wills 1540 and the Statute of Tenures 1660 was to give a free power of testamentary disposition. We have seen that the rule against perpetuities is designed to regulate or to prevent practices which would restrict the free alienation of land.

It follows that the law which regulates the modes in which landowners can exercise this power of alienation—the law of conveyancing—has always been an important part of the land law. It has had a long and complicated history; but at the present day the form required by law for the creation and transfer of estates and interests in land is both uniform and simple. Generally speaking one may say that, apart from dispositions by will, a deed, i.e. a sealed writing, is necessary, though leases in possession for not more than three years at the best rent obtainable without taking a premium may still be made without a deed and even by word of mouth. But an agreement evidenced by writing and for value, to confer an interest in land, is specifically enforceable in equity, and an attempted disposition for value by unsealed writing will be treated as equivalent to such an agreement. Moreover, even at common law a lease which ought to be made by deed but is not will not completely fail of effect, if possession is taken and rent paid under it; the tenant will be treated as tenant from year to year upon the terms of the lease so far as they are applicable to such a tenancy.

The trouble and expense involved in all dealings with land is still very great in the absence of any general provision for preserving any public record of title. Upon a sale of land the purchaser is normally entitled to have produced to him and to investigate the deeds recording previous transactions in the land going back for fifteen years (Law of Property Act 1969: formerly the period was thirty years); and though this period is sometimes reduced by agreement, the shortening of the period throws a risk on the purchaser, who is not only bound by all legal interests in the land which actually exist whether he discovers them or not, but also by all equitable interests which he would have discovered if he had insisted on an investigation for the longer period. Obviously no purchaser can, without expert assistance, make the investigation, of which the result will depend on the effect of numerous technical documents, such as settlements and mortgages. Supposing that the result of the investigation is satisfactory, and the purchase is completed, a subsequent purchaser must again go through the whole process; the results of each investigation are practically thrown away for the future. To do away with the evils of this system, as well as to guard against dangers of fraud and forgery, a Land Registry was established by the Land Transfer Act 1875, which was amended and extended by the Land Transfer Act 1897, both Acts being repealed and replaced by the Land Registration Acts 1925–1988.

The ideal of land registration is that a government office, after investigating the title, enters the applicant upon the register as owner, and furnishes him with a certificate in accordance with the entry; the entry is conclusive as to his right, and no further investigation of the previous title can subsequently be necessary. At every subsequent dealing with the land a new entry must be inserted on the certificate. One may compare such a public certification of the title with the stamp on a coin, which attests the genuineness of the metal, whereas the system of private investigation of title is as if a man was obliged to employ an expert analyst to test the genuineness of the coins which might be tendered to him. Such a system of registration has been found to work well in other countries, and there can be no doubt that it can, and will, be made universal with us. Though we have not yet attained a full system of compulsory registration, we may be said to be moving, surely and at an increasing pace, in that direction. Registration was made compulsory under the Act of 1897 in the Counties of London and Middlesex—now Greater London, as provided by the London Government Act 1963. The Land Registration Act 1925 exhibited an intelligible reluctance to hurry extension to other parts of the country until sufficient time had elapsed for testing the general effects of the property legislation of 1925. This period was fixed at ten years, and so it became possible, after the beginning of 1936, to extend compulsory registration to any county in England and Wales. Extension is now going forward on a large scale, delays being due partly to the necessity of thorough surveys, partly to the shortage of skilled staff. The compulsory system now covers virtually all built-up areas, and over 90 per cent of the total population of England and Wales. Since 1988 the register of title has been open to inspection by the general public. Parallel with this registration, under the Commons Registration Act 1965, the registration of common land and rights of common has now been completed.

12. *Settlements*

The way in which wealthy Englishmen have dealt with their capital has changed greatly in the last hundred and fifty years or so. At the beginning of the Victorian era, family property usually meant land. The concern of the wealthy landowner was to continue as long as possible the wealth and social status of the family. The law relating to family settlements was therefore concerned with the ways in which limited interests could be created in favour of various members of the family, stretching out as far as possible into the future. What had to be watched therefore was the perpetuity rule. There was no thought in those days of the Commissioners of Inland Revenue or of inheritance tax.

With the increase of industry and commerce in the nineteenth century, and especially with the development of joint stock companies with limited liability, investment in money rather than in land became the most convenient and popular form. Essentially such investments were of two types: either in fixed-interest securities, mainly Government stocks, or in stocks and shares of public companies on the Stock Exchange. Government stocks were safer. Interest payments were assured. And, above all to the Victorians, the capital was secure. The pound sterling maintained a steady value during the Victorian era, and in the then current atmosphere of British security and superiority the possibility of any erosion of the value of the pound was unthinkable. On the other hand, investment in shares of public companies quoted on the Stock Exchange ('equities') introduced the risk of dependence upon the fortunes of the company selected. There were bad times as well as good. Investment in equities involved risk. Such investments were not therefore available to trustees, without specific authorization. But large fortunes were made this way. The capitalist system needed investment of private capital to make it grow. It is only since 1945 that the inevitable inflation of the currency has led investors to think that 'equities' are safer than gilts; for they maintain a value even if the value of the currency deteriorates. And it is only in the slump of 1929–33, and more recently in 1973–5, 1987, and 1989, that catastrophic falls in Stock Exchange values have shown the vulnerability of equities, though after each such slump most equities have on the whole made very fair recoveries. These days the investor may often be uncertain where to turn, and there have been times when he might have done better to return to investment in land.

The development of the money economy and the decrease in the status attached to ownership of land led to change in the form of family settlements. No longer is the settlor trying to retain the family mansion and parkland in the family for ever.

He is trying to establish and retain a block of capital available for the members of his family for as long as he can do so. And now the main enemy is not the perpetuity rule, but fiscal legislation. It is no good to tie up the property by a series of limited interests for as long as the law will allow, if the bulk of the capital will have disappeared to the Revenue authorities in the meantime. The main problem of the present-day settlor is so to draft the limitations of the settlement as to attract the least amount of income tax and inheritance tax. To achieve this end, a wide and detailed knowledge of fiscal legislation and tax-planning technique is required. Only the most general comments will be made here. In order to understand the changes which have taken place in the practice relating to family settlements since the Victorian days, a brief description will follow, first of the standard form of eighteenth-century settlement of land, and then an outline of a modern tax-saving settlement.

(1) *Settlements of land.* We have seen that landowners have from early times sought methods of retaining their land in the family. It must be protected against spendthrift or incompetent successors, against creditors and moneylenders, against improvident sales, and, until the Forfeiture Act 1870, against forfeiture for treason. These objectives could be achieved by ensuring that no member of the family is ever capable of alienating the fee simple. A series of limited interests makes the alienation of the land very difficult, and, if skilfully done, impossible.

The most sophisticated method of tying up land in strict settlement developed in the seventeenth and eighteenth centuries. Possession of the land was to follow the normal order of succession to land, as would a hereditary title if one existed in the family. Provision needed to be made for dowager widows, and for younger sons and for daughters, and perhaps for other persons. All this could be done by giving a life estate to the head of the family; with the remainder to his sons successively in tail-male, with remainder to the daughters in tail, subject to a rentcharge in favour of the life tenant's widow upon his death, and in favour of any other persons desired to be benefited; and with power to the trustees to create long leases in the property for the purpose of charging the lease in order to provide portions for younger sons and daughters who did not inherit the land. Thus the property was tied up for a generation.

Upon the death of the life tenant, his eldest son, the remainder-man, would then be tenant in tail in possession. He would be able, provided that he was of age, to bar the entail and dispose of the fee simple. In order to avoid this situation, the practice was to effect a resettlement each generation. This was done upon the eldest son attaining the age of 21 years. He then became able to bar the entail, but, being tenant in tail remainder only, he could only effect a total bar by disentailing with the consent of his father, the tenant in possession. By an arrangement between father and son, a disentailment could be effected; but not so as to alienate the fee; rather to reduce the son's interest to a life estate in remainder, with remainder to his issue successively in tail. He could be compensated by an annuity charged upon the land. The limitations are then to the father for life, remainder to the son for life, remainder to the son's issue successively in tail, and subject to terms concerning rentcharges and portions as desired. The land is then tied up for another generation. This procedure, carried out each generation, could tie up the land indefinitely. The system was not obnoxious to the perpetuity rule, because each settlement and resettlement was designed to comply with the rule, and the perpetuity period began afresh from the time of each resettlement.

The industrial and commercial expansion of the nineteenth century required land to be available for development. Profits were available for landowners who were willing to develop the land by opening coal-mines, building factories, or developing in other ways. It was not possible to raise the necessary capital, or to sell or grant a long lease to developers, where the only marketable title was the life estate of the head of the family. This would be the situation pending a resettlement. It was in the interest of the public and of the landowners to make land freely alienable.

This was effected by the Settled Land Acts 1882 and 1925. The problem, in short, was to find a system where the landowner could continue to create all the beneficial interests he wished in favour of members of the family, and at the same time would be able to deal with the land, by sale, long lease or mortgage, as if he were a sole owner. The dilemma was solved by the principle of overreaching. The Settled Land Act 1882 provided that the tenant for life should have power to sell, grant leases, or mortgage the land, giving to the purchaser, lessee, or mortgagee a title free from the beneficial interests under the settlement. Capital money was, however, always to be paid, not to the life tenant, but to trustees, who were to hold the money upon the same trusts as those upon which the land had been held. Thus, on sale, the purchaser got a clear title from the tenant for life, free from the limitations of the settlement. The beneficiaries lost their interests in (say) £100,000 worth of land, but received exactly the same interests in £100,000 of money. The transaction is regarded as a change of investment. The policy was continued, with a number of amendments, in the 1925 legislation. Thus all land, however 'tied up' it may be by complex entails and other interests, has since 1882 been alienable by the tenant for life under his statutory powers.

Much the same result could be achieved by creating a trust for sale of the land; that is to say, by conveying the land to trustees upon trust to sell, and to hold the income of the land until sale, and the proceeds of sale, upon trust for beneficiaries in any desired order. Here the overreaching principle is clear. The beneficial interests are attached to the proceeds of sale. And, further, the equitable doctrine of Conversion operates, treating as done that which ought to be done, to effect a notional conversion in equity of the land into the proceeds of sale. Since 1925 the same interests can be created in personalty as in realty, and all the beneficial interests which can be created under a settlement can similarly be created behind a trust for sale.

We have seen that settled land is always alienable by the tenant for life. He sells or retains as he thinks fit. Under a trust for sale the trustees obviously can sell, and they are given by statute a discretionary power to retain. Thus the two procedures are alternative methods of creating settlements of land. The trust for sale has the enormous advantage of being available also for trusts of personalty, or of mixed land and personalty, and is also more convenient for creating discretionary trusts, which of course have no life tenant. The strict settlement method is rarely used at the present day. But many older titles are still dependent upon an understanding of its conveyancing procedures.

(2) *Modern Settlements.* A modern settlement, which will usually be of personalty or of mixed fund of land and personalty, will be designed so as to attract the lowest possible tax liability. The income of a trust is liable to income tax at the rate applicable to the beneficiary to whom the income is paid. Thus lower rates will be payable if the income is paid to beneficiaries with low incomes. Capital gains tax is payable by the trustees when investments are sold, or when the trust is terminated in whole or in part, and a beneficiary becomes entitled absolutely against the trustees to some property within the settlement. Inheritance tax is payable on property which passes on a death, other than from a husband to a wife or vice versa. Property passing on a death is defined in the Finance Act 1894, as amended by the Finance Act 1969, and includes: property owned absolutely by the deceased, property given away by the deceased within seven years of death, and property in which the deceased owned a limited interest within seven years of his death. Thus, on the death of a life tenant the property passes and inheritance tax becomes payable upon the capital value of the fund in which the deceased held his interest. For the purpose of establishing the rate at which inheritance tax is payable, all property (with certain exceptions) passing on the death is aggregated together. It will be obvious that the old-fashioned strict settlement, containing a series of life and other limited interests, is poorly designed for inheritance tax purposes.

In order, therefore, to avoid inheritance tax, the settlor should make the settlement seven years before his death, and the settlement should be designed to benefit the beneficiaries without giving limited interests to them. These requirements were substantially met before 1969 by the creation of discretionary trusts, by which property is given to trustees upon trust to apply the income on capital in favour of such one or more members of a group of beneficiaries as the trustees shall in their absolute discretion determine. None of the beneficiaries has any interest in the property—except in respect of income on capital actually paid to him. Until 1969 no property passed upon the death of a member of a class of beneficiaries under a discretionary trust, and no estate duty (the precursor of inheritance tax) was therefore payable for the duration of the trust. This was too wide a loophole for the tax planners: no wonder inheritance tax is called a voluntary tax. The Finance Act 1969 provided, in effect, that on the death of a beneficiary what in 1974 became capital transfer tax, and by the Finance Act 1986 inheritance tax, should be payable upon the proportion of the capital which corresponded to the proportion of the income which the deceased had received within a certain period before his death (usually seven years). Payments of capital do not attract inheritance tax liability, except in so far as income earned by the fund has not been paid out. To the extent that income has been retained, payments out are treated as income. Thus discretionary trusts have lost many of their fiscal advantages. Their flexibility, however, enables the trustees to make payments in a manner most suited to all the circumstances, including especially the needs of individual beneficiaries and the fiscal situation.

It is not possible here to say more about the different types of trust which are commonly created at the present time, nor of the powers and duties of the trustees, nor of the methods of administration. Specialist books on these topics need to be consulted. A wide variety of choice of settlement is available. The individual settlor must express his wishes to his legal advisors, and they will recommend the most appropriate type of trust to meet the particular situation. The main point to understand here is that different types of trust are designed to meet different situations. The past century has seen the standard form of family trust change from the old strict settlement based on successive limited interests and designed to keep specific land in the family, to the discretionary trust of personalty designed to give no interest to anybody for inheritance tax purposes. No one can say what the next century will bring. Most recently the Law Commission in 1989 recommended replacement of the dual system of trusts for sale and Settled Land Act settlements by a new trust machinery applicable to all trusts of land. Trustees would hold the legal estate on trust with a power (though not a duty) to sell and a power to retain. As at present, they would be able to overreach equitable interests; and the Law Commission considers that the simplicity of such a new system would outweigh any possible disadvantages. It remains to be seen whether this suggestion will become law, but the only really confident prediction must be that so long as capitalism remains, trusts will continue to change and develop so as to meet changes in social conditions and the tax structure.

13. *Mortgages of land*

We have seen that, under the ordinary form of a mortgage of freehold land used before the Property Acts, the legal estate was conveyed to the mortgagee, so that at law he became the owner of the property; but that the mortgagor was treated by equity as the owner—he had an equity of redemption, which was an equitable estate in the land; and he could only be deprived of his equity of redemption in certain defined ways, e.g. by foreclosure or sale. To permit this method of mortgaging land to continue would have been quite contrary to the policy of the Property Acts, which is that the owner of property shall be able to convey to a purchaser a good legal title free from all equities affecting that property. The real owner, the mortgagor, could not convey any legal title because he had none; and the legal owner, the mortgagee, could only convey a title subject to the mortgagor's equity of redemption. For this reason the Property Acts have revolutionized the modes of creating mortgages and some of their legal effects.

A legal mortgage can now be effected in one of two ways:

(1) The mortgagor demises the land to the mortgagee for a term of years absolute, subject to a proviso that the term shall cease when the mortgagor repays the loan. If the mortgagor is a lessee for years he effects the mortgage by a sub-lease. A second legal mortgage can be created by leasing the land to the second mortgagee for a term longer by at least one day than the term limited to the first mortgagee.

(2) The mortgagor creates by deed a legal charge upon the land. Both these methods of creating a mortgage give the mortgagee a legal interest in the land. Other methods can be used if it is desired to give him only an equitable interest in the land. Thus if A borrows money from B, and deposits with B the title-deeds of his land as security for the loan, B has an equitable mortgage on A's land. In the case of such deposits the rule that writing is required for the creation of interests in land is dispensed with.

Whether a mortgage is legal or equitable, the mortgagee can enforce his security by applying to the court for an order for foreclosure. Upon proof of the mortgage the court will make an order for foreclosure *nisi*, under which an officer of the court is directed to find what is due for principal, interest, and costs, and the mortgagor is ordered to pay within six months from the time when the amount is certified. If he fails to do so, the mortgagee will be entitled to an order of foreclosure absolute, the effect of which will be to vest the mortgaged property in him absolutely, but at the same time to prevent him—even if the property should prove insufficient—from claiming payment from the mortgagor, except upon terms of giving him a fresh right to redeem. As an alternative to foreclosure, the court may direct a sale of the property, and this may be fairer to both parties, since any surplus upon such sale will belong to the mortgagor, while the mortgagee may still sue for any deficiency.

In order to redeem, the mortgagor must give six months' notice or pay six months' interest. He may apply to the court if his right to redeem is disputed. Without any application to the court, the mortgagee, if his mortgage is a conveyance of the legal estate or ownership, may take possession; but this course is hazardous, since he may be called upon in a redemption action to account strictly not only for profits actually received by him, but also for those which he might but for his default have received, and all such profits, so far as they exceed the interest due for the time being, must be set off against the principal. A mortgage may contain a clause giving the mortgagee a power of sale, and such a power (subject to certain conditions) is now implied in every mortgage made by deed. If the power is exercised, the proceeds are applicable in the same way as the proceeds of a sale ordered by the court, and the mortgagor will remain liable to pay any deficiency. A power for the mortgagee to appoint a receiver who will collect the rents and profits is also now implied in mortgages by deed. To appoint a receiver is more convenient for the mortgagee than taking possession. Since the receiver is the mortgagor's agent, the mortgagee is not responsible for the receiver's acts and defaults; and any surplus beyond the outgoings (including the receiver's remuneration) and the interest due must be paid over to the mortgagor, and will not go in reduction of the principal.

Mortgagor and mortgagee have each, while in possession, considerable powers of leasing land mortgaged by deed unless, in the case of the mortgagor, the deed excludes them.

The changes made in the form of a mortgage have led to great changes in the law as to the priority of successive mortgages on the same land. In outline the modern rules are as follows:

Mortgagees, whether legal or equitable, of a legal estate rank according to the date at which they have registered their charges under the Land Charges Act 1972. But this rule is not so simple as at first sight it looks, for it means, not that priority is gained by registration, but that it is lost through failure to register. If any mortgage, other than a mortgage accompanied by transfer of the title-deeds, is unregistered, it is void as against a subsequent mortgagee, whether he registers his mortgage or not. A mortgagee who takes the title-deeds cannot register, and his position as against that of a mortgagee whose mortgage is registrable and registered is at present, for lack of judicial decision, merely conjectural. The better opinion is that the pre-1926 priorities of the legal over the equitable estate, and of the earlier in time over the later, still apply, except in so far as they are abrogated by the provisions of the 1925 legislation.

In certain cases a prior mortgagee may make further advances to the mortgagor which will rank in priority to subsequent mortgages:

(i) If he had no notice of a subsequent mortgage when he made his further advances—but registration of a subsequent mortgage is equivalent to notice.

(ii) If the prior mortgage was made expressly to secure a current account or other further advances, and further advances are made by the prior mortgagee, he can hold the land as security for both the original loan and the further advances, unless he had notice of a subsequent mortgage—registration (except in certain special cases) is not equivalent to notice.

(iii) If the mortgage deed imposes an obligation on the mortgagee to make further advances he gets priority for these advances even though he had notice of a subsequent mortgage.

If the mortgage is a mortgage of the equitable estate, the priority of successive mortgagees depends upon the order in which they give written notice to the trustees or other persons holding the legal estate. This rule, which was formerly applicable only to equitable interests in choses in action and personal trust funds, now applies to equitable interests in all kinds of property.

In view of the complexity of many mortgage documents, and the burden of artificially high interest rates upon mortgagors, the Law Commission proposed in 1991 that the court should have the power to cancel or vary any term of a mortgage which contravenes principles of fair dealing; but legislation to implement this is still awaited.

14. *Goods*

The transfer of goods is most commonly made by merely handing them over, and such a transfer is equally effectual whether the transfer is for value or by way of gift. An unconditional contract for sale of goods which are specific and ready for delivery is sufficient to transfer the ownership without any delivery. When goods are on board ship, the indorsement and delivery of the bill of lading (which is an acknowledgement of receipt of the goods given by the master of the ship) transfers the ownership. Further, goods may be transferred without delivery by deed, and where the transaction is for value even by writing without seal. Such deeds or instruments as a rule require for their validity to be registered under the Bills of Sale Acts 1878 and 1882, which were passed to prevent persons from obtaining credit by continuing to remain in possession of goods when they had secretly transferred their interest in them to others. In recent years the courts have frequently granted an injunction to restrain a defendant to a civil action from disposing of any of his assets, or removing them from the jurisdiction of the court. A bill of sale is commonly used as a means of mortgaging goods (see p. 118), but it may also be used as an out-and-out conveyance. The property in British ships can only be transferred by means of a bill of sale which is registered in the shipping register.

There are a few exceptions to the general rule that no one can make a transfer of goods who is not the owner. A person who receives current coins for value and in good faith acquires a good right even from a thief. So too the Factors Act 1889 protects persons who receive goods in good faith and for value from a mercantile agent to whom goods have been entrusted by the owner for the purpose of being sold or pledged.

15. *Intangible personal property*

A patent is the exclusive right granted by the Crown of 'using, exercising, and vending' an invention. Such grants used to be based on the Statute of Monopolies 1623 which, while in general prohibiting the grant of monopolies, made an exception in favour of patents 'for the term of fourteen years or under for the sole working or making of any manner of new manufactures within the realm to the true and first inventor or inventors of such manufactures, which others at the time of making such letters patent and grants shall not use'. The general principles so established still apply, but the law has been extensively revised by the Patents Act 1977 and by the application of European Union law. The term of the grant is now twenty years, but the court may in certain circumstances extend this period. As a condition of obtaining the patent, the applicant must furnish a specification (which in all ordinary cases is open to public inspection), showing the nature of his invention and the method of carrying it into effect. A register of patents is kept at the Patent Office, and assignments and licences to use patents must be entered upon it. In some cases a patentee can be compelled to grant a licence to use his patent on reasonable terms.

Copyright, which under the Copyright, Designs, and Patents Act 1988 extends to every original literary, dramatic, musical and artistic work, including photographs, sculpture, and archi-tecture, means the sole right of producing or reproducing the work in any material form, and of performing or, in the case of a lecture, delivering it in public; it includes the sole right of translation and of converting a dramatic into a non-dramatic work, and vice versa, and of making gramophone records, movie films, television and cable programmes, and similar devices for the mechanical performance of the work. As a rule the right is first vested in the author, and continues for fifty years after his death; but in the case of photographs and gramophone records the original owner of the negative or plate is treated as the author, and the right lasts for fifty years from the time when the negative or plate was made. The right is personal property, and passes upon the death of the owner to the persons named in his will or entitled upon his intestacy. It is assignable in writing by the owner during his lifetime; but, in spite of any assignment or agreement made by the author, it will revert to his representatives twenty-five years after his death. In the age of computer-generated work there are some detailed copyright rules which cannot be described adequately in this book.

The right to registered trade marks grew out of the rules of common law and equity, under which a trader who passed off his goods upon the public as those of another was held liable to damages and an injunction at the suit of the latter. These rules still exist (see pp. 167–9), but they have been supplemented by statutory provisions which enable a trader to acquire by registration at the Patent Office the exclusive right to use a distinctive trade mark in connection with his goods. Under the Trade Marks Act 1994 three-dimensional shapes, sounds, and even smells can be registered. The right to an unregistered trade mark can be assigned only in connection with the goodwill of the business concerned, and comes to an end with that goodwill. If however a trade mark has been registered it is assignable without goodwill.

The transfer of interests in the National Debt and public funds and in the debts of municipal and other public authorities, and of debentures, stocks, and shares in companies, is governed by numerous statutes. Such interests cannot be transferred without writing, and in most cases a deed is required; in any case the transfer is not complete except by entry in the books of the Bank of England or of the body or company concerned.

Something has already been said as to the assignment of ordinary debts and 'choses in action'; and the law relating to negotiable instruments—bills of exchange, cheques, and promissory notes—will be dealt with in the next chapter.

16. *Trusts*

The reader who has followed what was said in the second chapter will already have appreciated the nature of the trust, one of the most characteristic institutions of English Law, and its enormous importance as a part of our law of property. The importance of trusts has been greatly increased by the Property Acts because, as we have seen, it is only by means of the trusts that future interests in land can now be created (see p. 98).

Except that trusts of land must be created by writing, a trust may be created by any sufficient expression of intention to create it, whether the legal ownership is transferred to another to hold as trustee or remains with the creator of the trust, who in that case will himself be the trustee. (It may be noted that equitable rights may themselves form the subject of a trust. A, who has an interest in property held by B upon trust for him, may hold that interest upon trust for D, or transfer it to C upon trust for D.) If, however, an attempt is made to create a trust by transfer to a trustee, but the transfer itself fails from a defect in form— where land, for instance, is transferred by unsealed writing, or the transfer of shares in a company has not obtained some necessary consent of the Treasury—the trust also will fail, unless the transaction is one made for value, a term which includes settlements or agreements for settlement in consideration of a contemplated marriage, but not of one already celebrated. So too an attempt to make a direct gift, which fails because the proper method of transfer is not employed, will not take effect as a trust. On the other hand, a trust will not fail because the intended trustee refuses to undertake it or, in the case of a trust created by will, dies before the testator. A disposition, as distinct from creation, of a trust, whatever its subject-matter, must be in writing, and the term 'disposition' includes a mandate by the beneficiary to his trustee to hold it on behalf of someone else.

Trusts arise not only by a direct expression of intention but also by an inference or implication which may or may not correspond to any actual intention. Thus an agreement for the sale of land makes the vendor a trustee, subject to the payment of the purchase money, for the purchaser. Upon a bequest to a trustee upon trust for a beneficiary who predeceases the testator, the trustee will hold the property for the benefit of the testator's representatives. A gratuitous transfer of property into the joint names of himself and another will be presumed to be made upon trust for the person transferring, unless there is something to show that a benefit to the transferee was intended; such intention will be presumed where the transfer is made by a father to his child. Again, a person who acquires property for his own benefit by taking advantage of his position as trustee will be treated as holding it for the benefit of those entitled under the trust.

When all the possible beneficiaries are of full age and under no disability (such as that of an infant or someone subject to a mental health order), they may put an end to the trust by requiring the trustee to transfer the property to them or to dispose of it according to their directions; and this is so in spite of any direction to the contrary in the settlement, such as a direction that payment is not to be made to a beneficiary until he reaches the age of 25.

The duties of a trustee may be indefinitely varied by the terms of the instrument which creates the trust, and may range from a mere duty to make a legal conveyance to the beneficiary at his request, and in the meantime to permit him to possess and enjoy the property, to extensive and onerous duties of management, sale, investment, and application of capital and income. Apart from certain exceptional cases, a trustee is entitled to no remuneration for his trouble, unless the terms of the trust so direct, and is liable not only for dishonest dealing with the trust property, but for all loss due either to non-observance of the directions in the settlement and the general rules of law, or to failure on his part to act up to the high standard of care which equity and statute law require of him. The range of permissible investments, for instance, is defined by statute in so far as the settlement makes no provision; but, even within the limits of investment allowed by statute or settlement, a trustee may incur liability by want of due care in exercising his discretion. Any failure of duty in a trustee, however innocent morally, is a breach of trust. In practice, however, and especially in the matter of investments, the older picture of an inexorable equity exercising unrelenting vigilance over the trustee's conduct is passing. It would be impossible to persuade anyone to act as trustee unless the discretion entrusted to him were very liberally conferred, and it is now possible for a trustee to delegate to an agent, not merely pieces of business requiring especial skill, but the whole business of the trust, and escape liability so long as he acts in good faith.

In cases of doubt a trustee may protect himself by obtaining, at the cost of the trust property, the direction of the court, and the Trustee Act 1925 enables the court to relieve a trustee, who has acted honestly and reasonably and ought fairly to be excused, from liability for breach of trust. The Variation of Trusts Act 1958 gives the court wide powers to vary trusts and sanction dealings with trust property in the interests of beneficiaries.

Upon the death or retirement of a trustee, the surviving trustees have, in the absence of any provision in the settlement, the power of appointing another in his place. The court also has a power to appoint new trustees and to remove a trustee for unfitness or misconduct.

The rights of the beneficiaries under a trust, as has already been seen, are interests in property closely analogous to legal interests, and but little inferior to them in security. Not only do they hold good against the trustee himself, and against his creditors during his lifetime and his representatives after his death, but also against all to whom he may have transferred the property, and who cannot show that they acquired it for value and without notice of the trust. Even where a trustee has misappropriated trust property the fund may still preserve its identity, and, so long as it can be identified, the rights of the beneficiaries will attach to the fund into whatever form it may have been converted by him. If he has used it to swell his bank balance, it will be presumed that, in drawing on that balance, he has drawn out his own money before touching trust money; if he has made an investment with trust money—even an investment which is itself a breach of trust—that investment is still trust property, to which the trustees' creditors have no claim.

We have seen that the difficulty of obtaining the gratuitous services of suitable persons to act as trustees has necessarily led to the practice of reposing an ever wider range of discretion in those who can only thus be persuaded to act. The present danger is perhaps not so much that an honest trustee may be unfairly penalized as that a dishonest trustee may with impunity inflict loss on the beneficiaries. The provision sometimes inserted in a settlement for giving remuneration to a professional man who is one of the trustees is open to considerable objection since it may give him an interest in incurring expense, and will in any case tend to make the other trustees leave the management mainly in his hands. An Act of 1906 instituted the office of Public Trustee. This officer may be appointed trustee under any will or settlement, either as a mere 'custodian' trustee, in whom the ownership of the trust property is vested, leaving the active duties to other trustees, or as an ordinary trustee, with powers and duties of management. Fees in proportion to the value are payable in respect of all property in the hands of the Public Trustee; but his remuneration, like that of other Government servants, is a fixed salary. The Consolidated Fund of the United Kingdom is liable to the beneficiaries for the acts and defaults of the Public Trustee and his subordinates. In recent years, however, the Public Trustee has only had a small and declining proportion of the total work of trusteeship and executorship (see p. 128), and in 1972 a Committee of Inquiry recommended that no new work should be taken on, and that the office be wound up and merged with that of the Official Solicitor. But this recommendation, accepted by the Government at the time, was later rejected by the Government in 1974. The Public Trustee's office therefore continues to discharge the work it retains, though the volume of this work is still declining, and the administration of the office was in 1988 combined with that of the Official Solicitor.

17. *Mortgages and pledges of personalty*

Mortgages can be made of chattels personal as well as of land. A mortgage of debts and of equitable interests in personalty can be made in the form of a conveyance by the mortgagor to the mortgagee with a proviso for redemption. The priority of successive mortgagees depends on the date when the mortgagee gives notice to the debtor or trustee. Mortgages of shares are usually made by depositing the share certificate with the lender. This, like a deposit of title-deeds in the case of land (see p. 109), creates an equitable mortgage. Priority, as between successive mortgagees of shares, is determined by the date at which the mortgages were effected, as a company is under no obligation to accept notices by mortgagees. A mortgage of tangible property is made by a deed, which is called a Bill of Sale; and, under the Bills of Sale Act 1882 (as modified by the Consumer Credit Act 1974), it must be in the form given in the schedule to the latter

Act, and attested and registered as required by that Act. It cannot be given in consideration of any sum under £30. The priority of successive mortgagees depends upon the order in which successive Bills of Sale are registered. The Bills of Sale Acts do not apply to documents accompanying transactions in which the possession of the chattels passes. Therefore they do not apply to pledges.

A *pledge* is a security upon goods created by the actual transfer of the possession of the goods themselves, or of such documents of title to goods as bills of lading, but without the conveyance of any legal ownership. A pledge carries with it a power of sale, but there is nothing corresponding to foreclosure. The business of pawnbrokers, which consists in lending money upon pledges of goods, is the subject of special statutory regulation.

18. *Liens*

The term *lien* is used in different senses. A common law or possessory lien is the right to retain goods, money, or documents which are in one's possession until payment of some claim due from the owner. It commonly arises in respect of services rendered in relation to the property, as in the case of the carriage of goods; but in some cases, like those of a solicitor and banker, the lien may be asserted in respect of the general balance due from the customer. An innkeeper has a lien for his charges upon the traveller's goods brought to the inn and, contrary to the usual rule, has by statute been given a power of sale over such goods. Liens of this kind, being mere rights of retention, are lost as soon as possession is given up.

The equitable lien of the vendor of land, who has conveyed the property without receiving payment of the purchase money, is quite independent of possession, and gives a right to have the property sold under an order of the court.

Maritime liens upon ships and cargoes are also in the nature of mortgages or charges independent of possession. They arise in respect of damage done by collision, and upon advances of money or the rendering of services, such as salvage, in times of emergency. Inasmuch as the later advance or service is beneficial to the holder of an earlier lien, it will as a rule rank in priority to it.

19. *Execution and bankruptcy*

When judgment has been obtained against a man in respect of any debt or liability, it will be enforced, if need be, by execution, i.e. the court will make an order, under which a sufficient part of the debtor's property is seized and sold or otherwise made available for payment. At one time execution might be made against the debtor's person, and he could be kept in prison indefinitely in default of payment. Since 1869 imprisonment for debt has been rare, and by the Administration of Justice Act 1970 it has been completely abolished, and replaced by the remedy of attachment of earnings, i.e. a procedure whereby a portion of the debtor's earnings may be directed by the court to be paid direct to the creditor.

When a person's property is insufficient for payment of his debts, it would obviously be unfair that the creditors who first obtain judgment and execution should be paid in full, leaving nothing to those who may try to enforce their claims later; nor is it desirable that a man should indefinitely remain under a load of debts which (it may be through no fault of his own) he is unable to meet. This is the justification of the law of bankruptcy, originally applicable only to traders, but now, with few exceptions, to all insolvent persons, and governed by the Insolvency Act 1986. A corporation cannot be made bankrupt; but a company formed under the Companies Act 1985 or similar earlier Acts can be wound up, and its property distributed, according to rules similar to those applicable to bankruptcy.

The debtor or a creditor presents his petition to the Bankruptcy Court of the district in which the debtor resides or carries on business—in London, the High Court; elsewhere, normally one of the County Courts. An act of bankruptcy must be proved, and under this term are included various acts, which show the debtor's insolvency or his intention to delay or defraud his creditors. If this is proved, the court makes a preliminary order, called a 'receiving order', which protects the debtor's property and prevents creditors from suing him without the leave of the court. The debtor may then (with the court's approval) make a composition or scheme of arrangement with his creditors; but if this is not done he will be adjudicated bankrupt, and the whole of his property (not including property of which he is himself a trustee, or the tools of his trade and the necessary clothing and bedding of himself and his family) will vest in the 'official receiver' (a public officer) or some other trustee, and become divisible among his creditors who prove their debts. Rates and taxes, wages of clerks and servants, and some other claims are, within limits, paid in preference to others, and the rights of secured creditors, such as mortgagees, are not prejudiced by the bankruptcy; but in general the distribution will be made rateably. Voluntary settlements (in particular family settlements made after marriage) are set aside by a bankruptcy if made within two years before; and even if made within ten years before, unless it is shown that at the time the bankrupt was able to meet his liabilities without the settled property.

At any time after adjudication a bankrupt may apply to the court for his discharge, which, if granted, will enable him to start again, stripped of his property, but (with certain exceptions) free from any claim which might have been proved against him in the bankruptcy. But the discharge may be refused or postponed if he has been guilty of certain offences or misconduct in connection with the bankruptcy, or if his assets are insufficient for the payment of 50p in the £, unless this is shown not to be due to the debtor's fault.

20. *Wills*

A testator had, before 13 July 1939, an unlimited power of disposition by will over all his proprietary rights which survive him, including, since 1925, an entailed interest in possession. But on and after that date the Inheritance (Family Provision) Act 1938 gives to the dependants of a testator, and the Intestates'

Estates Act 1952 gives to those of an intestate, power to apply to the court for a reasonable maintenance out of the estate, if such is not provided by the will, or the law of intestacy, or the combined operation of will and law where the intestacy was only partial. The 1938 Act was repealed and replaced by the Inheritance (Provision for Family and Dependants) Act 1975, which increases the range of dependants who may apply for provision on death and gives the court wider powers than previously existed so that it can make whatever type of order may be most appropriate in the circumstances. Dependants are defined in the 1975 Act as a wife or husband; a former spouse who has not remarried; a child of the deceased (including an illegitimate or adopted child); a person who was treated by the deceased as a child of the family in relation to any marriage of the deceased (e.g. a child of the deceased's wife by a former marriage); and any other person who was being wholly or partly maintained by the deceased immediately before his death. To qualify in this last category a dependant need not have been related to the deceased, and thus a mistress would be included. Furthermore, there is no qualifying period during which the applicant must have received maintenance from the deceased. 'Maintained' means that the deceased was making a substantial contribution in money or money's worth towards the reasonable needs of the applicant, and he did not receive full valuable consideration for this: thus food and shelter are included in the definition. The court may attach to its grant such conditions as it sees fit. The maintenance ordered may be in the form of a lump sum, by way of periodical payments of income, or by transfer or settlement of specific property, or the variation of a settlement. Such payments to a spouse will normally end if he or she remarries, but the original provisions in the 1938 Act excluding a child from further benefit on attaining the age of majority or on marriage have been repealed by the 1975 Act. The court must take into consideration the nature of the testator's property, the pecuniary position of the dependant, his or her conduct to the testator, and any other relevant circumstance, and the testator's reasons for the dispositions made by him in his will.

For the making of a will compliance with the following formalities is now necessary:

(1) The will must be in writing.
(2) It must be signed by the testator or by some person in his presence and by his express direction.
(3) The signature must be made or acknowledged by the testator in the presence of two or more witnesses, both present at the same time.
(4) The witnesses must attest and sign the will in the testator's presence, or acknowledge their signatures in his presence.

A soldier or airman on active service, or mariner at sea, can make an informal will, even by word of mouth, which will be valid provided that his communication to his audience was not a mere statement, but a request to him to see his intention carried out. The Administration of Justice Act 1982 also sets out the form of an international will recognized as formally valid in all countries subscribing to the Convention on International Wills.

Any legacy or benefit given by the will to a witness or to a witness's wife or husband was formerly void, though the will as a whole was unaffected. But the Wills Act 1968 provides that if a will is already duly executed with two other qualified witnesses, the attestation of any person who would have been caught by this rule must be disregarded.

A testator can revoke his will at any time during his life. But breach of a contract not to revoke it will subject his estate to a claim for damages. Furthermore, if two parties (usually, but not necessarily, husband and wife) make 'mutual wills', with identical ultimate beneficiaries, the death of one of the parties without alteration of his will may have the effect of binding the survivor to make no alteration, in the sense that a trust will arise, under which the terms of the will must be fulfilled.

A will is revoked

(1) By the marriage of the testator, unless it appears from the will that at the time it was made the testator was expecting to be married to a particular person, and that he intended that the will

(or a particular disposition in the will) should not be revoked by that marriage, and that marriage takes place.

(2) By the making of a new will or of a codicil or other writing executed with the same formalities as a will, so far as such later document is inconsistent with the will. A codicil is really a supplementary will, and is generally used for making some alteration in a will without revoking it as a whole.

(3) By burning, tearing, or otherwise destroying a will, if this is done by the testator or any person in his presence and by his direction with the intention of revoking it.

(4) A complete and intentional obliteration of a will or any part of it, so that what was written can no longer be seen, amounts to a revocation of what is obliterated; but merely striking words through with a pen or altering them has no effect, unless the cancellation or alteration is signed by the testator and attested by two witnesses like a new will. Where, after a testator has made a will, his marriage is dissolved or annulled, the will takes effect as if any appointment of the former spouse as an executor were omitted, and any devise or bequest to such former spouse lapses.

The accidental loss or destruction of a will has no effect upon its validity, and its contents may be proved by the production of copies or drafts, or even by the recollection of persons who have seen it or heard it read.

Bequests of real estate are technically known as devises, bequests of personalty as legacies. A legacy may be specific, i.e. given in terms which show that a particular thing and no other is meant (e.g. 'my only gold watch', 'my Oxford City stock'). A legacy which earmarks, not a particular thing, but a particular fund or collection out of which it is to come (e.g. 'one of my three violins') is called demonstrative. A legacy which earmarks neither thing nor collection (e.g. 'a violin', '£500') is called general. A bequest of the surplus is called residuary. A specific bequest will fail if the testator parts with the thing before death. But a demonstrative legacy, if the fund out of which it is to come ceases to exist before the death, becomes payable as a general legacy. Devises are of two kinds only, specific and residuary. The interests of all persons who take under a will can take effect only after payment of the debts of the deceased. Under the Administration of Estates Act 1925, real and personal estates are equally liable to the payment of these debts.

Under the Administration of Justice Act 1982, where a will contains a devise or bequest to a child or remoter descendant of the testator, and the intended beneficiary dies before the testator, leaving issue who are living at the time of the testator's death, then, unless a contrary intention appears in the will, the devise or bequest passes to the issue living at the testator's death. For the purposes of this provision such issue include illegitimate children and any persons conceived before the testator's death and born living thereafter.

When a bequest fails through the death of the person for whom it was intended, and does not pass under a residuary bequest, as must necessarily be the case if the bequest which fails is itself residuary, the property will be dealt with as upon an intestacy.

21. *Intestacy*

Before 1926, when a person died wholly or partly intestate, the distribution of his property differed widely according as it was real or personal estate. The real estate descended to the heir in accordance with rules laid down by statutes of 1833 and 1859. The personal estate was distributed in accordance with rules laid down by the Statutes of Distribution of Charles II's and James II's reigns. The Administration of Estates Act 1925 has repealed the Statutes of Distribution altogether, and has confined the operation of the statutes of 1833 and 1859 to three specific cases.[3] This Act has been further amended by the Family Provision Act 1966. Apart from these cases, the entire property, other than that in which the deceased's interest ceased at his death, is held by the executors or administrators on trust for sale, in the first instance for the payment of his debts, and then for distribution as laid down in the Intestates' Estates Act 1952, which has replaced the relevant provisions of the Act of 1925. Since, however, cases concerning property which has devolved according to the 1925 Act provisions will for many years continue to come before the courts, they are summarized in a note at the end of the book.[4]

The present rules are:

(1) *Rights of surviving spouse.* He or she takes—

(i)   All the personal chattels (that is chattels such as furniture, motor cars, and articles of household or personal use or ornament, but not chattels used for business purposes).

(ii)   If there is issue, £125,000, free of inheritance tax.

(iii) If there is no issue, £200,000, free of inheritance tax.

(iv)   If there is issue, a life interest in half the remaining estate, which may, at his or her option, be redeemed for a capital payment. The other half, and the reversion in the first half, are held on the 'statutory trusts' for the issue.

(v)   If there is no issue, but there are parents or, failing them, brothers and sisters of the whole blood, then the spouse takes half the remaining estate absolutely, the other half going to parents, or being held on the 'statutory trusts' for brothers and sisters, as the case may be.

(vi)   The claims of the spouse override absolutely those of all relations remoter than those mentioned in (v).

(vii) Where part of the estate consisted of a 'matrimonial home', i.e. a house in which the surviving spouse was resident at the time of the death, the spouse may normally require the representatives to appropriate the deceased's interest in the house in or towards the satisfaction of his or her absolute interest in the estate.

The phrase 'statutory trusts' calls for some explanation. The term 'issue' includes not only children, but also the children of children who have predeceased the intestate. The scheme is that these take an 'absolutely vested interest' only on the attainment of 18 years or marriage. Until then the property is held in trust for them. Should a child die before attaining an absolutely vested interest, his interest passes on to those next entitled, that is to say, other children, a parent, brothers and sisters of the whole blood, a surviving spouse, or remoter relatives if there is no surviving spouse. The personal representatives have the powers to maintain and advance children given to trustees by the Trustee Act 1925. In order to equal the shares of the children, any sum paid by the intestate to a child by way of advancement or on the marriage of the child must be brought into account. An advancement means a sum of money paid to a child to start him in business or to make a permanent provision for him; it does not include casual payments given as a present or to help to tide over temporary difficulties.

The interests of the children, if there is no surviving spouse, absolutely override those of any other relatives. Under the Children Act 1975 an adopted child has the same right to succeed on the intestacy of his adoptive parent as any other child born to that parent.

(2) *Rights of parents.* Where there are no issue and no surviving spouse, the parents, if both are alive, take the property in equal shares. If only one is alive, that parent takes all.

(3) *Rights of brothers and sisters of the whole blood.* If spouse, issue, and parents are all lacking, the property is held on the statutory trusts for brothers and sisters of the whole blood, or the children of deceased members of that class.

(4) *Rights of remoter relatives.* It must be emphasized that relatives remoter than parents, or brothers or sisters of the whole blood, and children of such brothers and sisters deceased, can succeed to no part whatever of the estate, if there is a surviving spouse. If there is no spouse, they take in the following order, (i) brothers and sisters of the half blood; (ii) grandparents in equal shares; (iii) uncles and aunts, who are brothers and sisters of the whole blood of a parent of the intestate; (iv) uncles and aunts who are brothers or sisters of the half blood of a parent of the intestate. Class (ii) take the property absolutely. In the case of Classes (i), (iii), and (iv) the property is held on the statutory trusts, as in the case of issue. Thus, just as grandchildren can

take, so can nephews and nieces and first cousins. But, in the case of these classes, the rule relating to the bringing into account of advances does not apply.

22. *Executors and administrators*

Even if a will does not give property to trustees, the property, whether real or personal, does not go directly to those for whose benefit it is given, nor does property passing on intestacy go directly to those entitled under the rules above stated. It vests in the first instance in 'personal representatives', namely the executor appointed by the will or, where there is no will or no executor appointed under the will, the administrator—usually a person interested in the property—appointed by the court. The Public Trustee may be appointed as executor or administrator.

The executor or administrator, whose duties in many ways resemble those of a trustee, must in the first instance discharge the funeral expenses, the cost (including the payment of inheritance tax) of obtaining probate of the will or 'letters of administration', and the debts of the deceased. It is only after these claims are discharged that the executor or administrator will transfer the property to those entitled; or, if the property is settled by will and the executor is not himself trustee, to trustees for them. In many cases, as where the persons entitled are not of age, or not yet in existence, or not to be found, an executor or administrator will have to retain the property in his hands for a considerable time, though he may sometimes relieve himself by a payment or transfer into court, and in any case he can obtain the direction of the court when doubts arise as to the proper course which he should take.

6 Contracts

1. *Acts in the law*

To a large class of acts, conveniently comprised in the term 'acts in the law', the law gives an effect which corresponds more or less completely with the intention of the person who acts. A purchaser of goods, for instance, desires to become the owner, or to have the right to become the owner of them, and is willing to be bound to pay for them, and this is precisely the legal consequence which the law attaches to his agreement to purchase.

For the most part an act in the law will require for its full effect the concurrence of more persons than one, since a man can hardly alter his own legal position without affecting that of another or others. A man cannot be compelled against his will to accept even a benefit. Thus a gift or legacy will fail if the intended recipient refuses to take it. Yet there is a special sense in which we may properly distinguish one-sided or 'unilateral' transactions from those which are two-sided or 'bilateral'. If a man should make a gratuitous promise to pay £100 to another, his promise, though made without the knowledge of the other, will, if made in the proper form, be so far binding on him that he cannot revoke it, though it is true that the other may repudiate the benefit and thus release him. But the promisor in the meantime is bound. Such a transaction is unilateral. On the other hand, where a transaction would impose on each party both benefit and a burden, as in the case of a sale, neither will be bound until both are bound: until that moment is reached, either can withdraw. Such transactions are bilateral.

2. *Conveyance and contract*

Among acts in the law we must sharply distinguish in principle the two types of conveyance and contract. In the case of a conveyance the effect of the transaction is, so to speak, exhausted as soon as the transaction is complete, and no special relation remains outstanding between the parties. A gift makes the recipient owner of the thing given as fully as the giver was previously. The giver must respect his proprietary rights; but this duty is no more than what is owed by everyone else. The new owner has no rights against the giver which he has not against all the world. Such a transaction is purely a conveyance. On the other hand an agreement by which one man agrees to serve another who undertakes to pay him wages creates between them special duties of the kind technically known as obligations, duties which at least in the first instance can be enforced only by and against the parties to the transaction. Such a transaction is the purest type of what in English law is called a contract.

Clear as is the distinction in principle between these two types, we shall find that many, if not most, ordinary transactions contain elements belonging to both, and the assignment of a transaction to one class or the other is sometimes a matter of difficulty, and cannot always be made in accordance with strict logic. An agreement for the purchase of land seems at first sight to be purely a contract; it gives the purchaser not the ownership of the land, but a right to be made owner, while it imposes on him the duty of paying the purchase-money. But it amounts to an 'estate contract', registrable under the Land Charges Act 1972 (see Chapter 5, note 1). Its due registration turns it into a proprietary interest, enforceable against everybody. If the purchaser fails to register, his interest is still good against a subsequent donee of the land, or even a purchaser of an equitable interest in it, but void against a purchaser of the legal estate 'for money or money's worth'. Again, when the agreement is completed by a formal conveyance, some special duties may remain incumbent on the seller to make good any defects in the title. A lease is mainly a conveyance and is classed as such in that it gives the tenant a right to the land, which, during the tenancy, is good against all the world; yet the tenant's covenants for payment of rent, or to keep the premises in repair, are essentially contractual obligations. A sale of goods is mainly a contract; yet many sales of goods immediately transfer the ownership to the buyer and give him rights against the world at large.

For practical purposes of classification, however, it is as a rule not difficult to place a transaction in one class or the other according as it corresponds more or less completely with one type or the other. Of conveyances something has been said in connection with the law of property; they are different for different classes of property, and in many cases subject to special requirements of form. Contracts on the other hand, while infinitely various in their subject-matter, have much in common as regards their formation and the conditions of their validity. It must be remembered that much that will here be said of contracts, especially when we come to speak of the effects of mistake, fraud, misrepresentation, or illegality, is equally true, or true with variations, of conveyances in so far as their force, like that of contracts, depends on agreement.

3. *Formal contracts*

A contract may be described as a transaction which consists wholly or mainly of a legally binding promise or set of promises. No promise is binding in our law unless it either satisfies certain requirements of form or is given for valuable consideration. Though classed among formal contracts the so-called 'contracts of record', which owe their force to an entry in the records of a Court of Justice, are for the most part not contracts at all. A person who has had a judgment given against him has not really contracted or promised, though he is bound to satisfy the judgment. Yet occasionally, as where a judgment is entered by consent as the result of a compromise, the judgment does embody a real agreement, and we may in such cases see a genuine contract deriving force from its judicial form. So too in the case of a recognizance, which is a promise made to the Crown to pay a sum of money in the event, for instance, of an accused person failing to surrender for trial.

But the commonest kind of formal contract is the contract by deed, sometimes known as a specialty. The promises contained in such a document are known as covenants. The formality of sealing, which served as a test of genuineness in former days when illiteracy was common in all classes and handwritings hard to distinguish, is abolished by the Law of Property (Miscellaneous Provisions) Act 1989, but to become operative a deed must be signed and witnessed, and needs to be 'delivered'. Delivery is formally made by using some such words as 'I deliver this as my act and deed', in the presence of another, and handing the document to him; but any acts or words which sufficiently show an intention that the document should take effect are sufficient. A delivery may be made conditionally, i.e. it may be accompanied by a declaration that the deed shall take effect only when some condition is fulfilled, and a deed so delivered is called an escrow.

4. *Consideration*

The main use of a deed for purposes of contract is to enable a man to bind himself by a gratuitous promise. A promise to pay money, or to perform a service, or confer any benefit, unless made by record or by deed, has no binding force if the promisor gets no 'consideration' for the promise. The consideration is an act or forbearance of the other party, or the promise of some act or forbearance, accepted by the promisor in return for his promise. Thus, in a sale of goods, the supply of the goods, or the promise to supply them, will be a consideration for the promise to pay; and the promise to pay, or a cash payment, will be the consideration for the promise to supply them. Whether the consideration is of any actual value, or actually benefits the promisor, is immaterial. The delivery of the most trivial object by A to B, or the doing of a trivial act at B's request, may be a consideration for B's promise to pay A a large sum of money.

The makers of a remedy for influenza offered by advertisement £100 to anyone who should use it for a specified period and contract the disease. A lady who so used it, and caught influenza, was held to have furnished the consideration for the promise. It is enough, but it is essential, that the promisor has got something which he had not got before, and which he had no legal right to require. A promise made in return for a previous service is not binding; 'a past consideration' is no consideration, for the promisor gets nothing for his promise which he had not got already. So again the doing, or the promise to do something for X which one is already bound to do for X, is no consideration for any promise by X. If I owe Z £100 today, and he undertakes, if I will pay him £50 now, to let me off the rest of the debt, his undertaking is legally unenforceable, for he was already entitled to the £50, though, by a rule derived from Equity, I may well have a good defence to any action brought against me later for the balance if I rely upon Z's promise to waive my existing legal obligation to him. So too when a person is under a public duty his performance of the duty is no consideration, as where a policeman in discharge of his duty furnishes information for which a reward has been offered. The reward cannot be recovered unless the policeman can show that in some way he has rendered a service outside his duty. Nor is the abstention, or promise to abstain, from unlawful conduct consideration for any promise. An act, or the promise of an act, which is unlawful, or even immoral in a sense recognized by law, not only is no consideration, but will even vitiate a transaction in which some other sufficient consideration is present.

5. *Offer and acceptance*

The formation of a contract commonly proceeds by way of offer and acceptance. One man will propose to another to make a promise to him, asking in return for the doing of some act or the making of a counter-promise. Such a proposal is called an offer. In itself it has no binding effect on either side, and may be withdrawn at any moment before it has been accepted. It will fail if more than a reasonable time elapses before it is accepted, or if either party dies before acceptance. Even an express declaration that the offer shall remain open until a certain time will not be binding unless it was made by deed, or something was given as a consideration for it, as in the case of Stock Exchange options. The most that such a declaration can do is to make sure that, unless revoked, the offer shall not fail from mere lapse of time before the time specified, nor continue open afterward. If the offer is accepted it is converted into a binding promise. The acceptance may be made by words written or spoken, or by conduct showing an intention to accept. If a counter-promise is proposed as the consideration, the acceptance amounts to a giving of the counter-promise; if the consideration is to consist of the doing of an act the acceptance will consist of the doing of the act: e.g. A offers a reward for the furnishing of information; B supplies the information, and thereby at the same moment supplies the consideration asked for by A and converts A's offer into a binding promise.

Neither an offer nor its revocation can be made without communication to the other party. If one man should offer by advertisement to pay £1,000 for a rare book, and another, not knowing of the offer, should happen to send him a copy of the book at the price, there would be no contract, for the offer was never made to him. Similarly, one to whom an offer has been made, so long as it has not lapsed, is entitled to treat it as open until he has actually received notice that it is revoked. On the other hand, communication is not necessary for the acceptance of an offer. The offer may, of course, prescribe communication as essential to a valid acceptance. But it may often be inferred from the nature of the offer, and the circumstances under which it is made, that actual communication is not required. This is commonly the case where acceptance is to be made by doing an act. An automatic machine placed in a public place is a standing offer on the part of the company which puts it there of promises to supply articles in return for the act of placing a coin in the machine. Every person who puts in a coin accepts the offer, and imposes on the company the duty of supplying the promised article. So too the lady who unsuccessfully used the influenza remedy was held to have thereby converted the makers' offer into a promise, though her very existence was at the time of her doing so unknown to them. In the case of contracts made by correspondence, our courts have laid down the rule that the posting of a letter of acceptance is a complete acceptance, even if the letter is lost in the post. It follows that a revocation will be inoperative if it does not reach the acceptor before his acceptance is posted. On the other hand, where the communication can be said to be instantaneous, for instance by telephone, teleprinter, or fax, the contract is complete only when the acceptance is actually communicated to the offeror. In a case of 1955 the question to be determined was the locality of completion. The offer was made by teleprinter in London, accepted by teleprinter in Amsterdam. It was held that the contract was made in London.

6. *Written contracts*

Contracts other than formal contracts are commonly called simple or parol contracts. The latter phrase, meaning 'oral', was used in contradistinction to deeds, inasmuch as our early law paid no attention to writing unless it was authenticated by seal. Writing is, however, required by statute for the validity of some contracts, and the enforceability of others. The cases fall into two categories, in neither of which is the necessity for consideration dispensed with. (*a*) Some contracts, for instance, contracts of marine insurance, and contracts with moneylenders for repayment of money lent, must be *in writing*, otherwise they will be void. The most significant addition to this group has been made by the Law of Property (Miscellaneous Provisions) Act 1989, under which contracts for the sale or other disposition of land must be made in writing and signed by all parties to the contract. It is now no longer possible, therefore, to make an oral contract for the sale of land. (*b*) Some others must *either* themselves be in writing *or* have some note or memorandum in writing, signed by 'the party to be charged' or his agent. The statutory provisions laying down these requirements were in the Statute of Frauds 1677, s. 4. Unlike the Acts governing contracts which fall within category (*a*) they do not affect the validity of the contracts to which they apply, but only prescribe that without the written note or memorandum, which may be made at any time before an action is brought on the contract, they are incapable of proof. Moreover, if 'the party to be charged' (the defendant) has signed, it is immaterial that the other party has not signed. The only part of the Statute of Frauds, s. 4, which has survived the Law Reform (Enforcement of Contracts) Act 1954, is that which applies the requirement of the written memorandum to a contract of guarantee, for instance of a friend's overdraft at his bank.

Two other types of contract may be conveniently mentioned in this section: (*a*) Under the Contracts of Employment Act 1972, as subsequently re-enacted by the Employment Protection Act 1975, employers must supply written particulars of the terms of their employment to any employees whose normal hours of employment are at least twenty-one hours each week. A failure to conform to such a requirement is a criminal offence, and so most such contracts will now in practice be in writing, even though the Act makes no such direct obligation upon employers. (*b*) It has become increasingly common in this century for goods to be purchased by means of a hire-purchase agreement, that is, a contract whereby the seller relinquishes possession of the goods forthwith to a customer who agrees to pay for the goods by instalments. But the property in the goods does not pass to the customer until the final instalment has been paid. Under the common law it was possible for a seller to fix an instalment price which appeared to be small, but which in fact resulted in a total price far in excess of the listed cash price. Also it was possible so to frame the agreement that the seller could reclaim the goods and retain all money already paid when any default was made by the purchaser in the payment of a single instalment. But now, under the Fair Trading Act 1973 and the Consumer Credit Act 1974, replacing the earlier Hire-Purchase Acts 1938 and 1964, considerable protection has been provided for the purchaser in any case of a hire-purchase agreement where the total purchase price does not exceed £5,000.

The Director General of Fair Trading has overall supervision in the whole field of consumer credit, and is empowered to initiate legal proceedings against suppliers who may be in breach of specific rules laid down. The Consumer Credit Act 1974 provides for a uniform system applying to all forms of credit agreements. Among the many details of the system it may be noted that a hire-purchase contract must be in writing, and signed by both parties. In most cases the hirer must be given a copy of the document he signs immediately after signature, and another copy must be delivered or sent to him within seven days thereafter. If the document was signed other than at 'appropriate trade premises', the hirer has the right to cancel the contract within four days after receiving the second of these statutory copies (a provision mainly designed to protect housewives from unscrupulous doorstep salesmen). The hirer may also, in any case and at any time, terminate the agreement on payment of the instalments already due, together with such sum, if any, as will make the total payment not less than one-half of the total hire-purchase price, unless a lesser sum is specified in the contract. If the hirer is in default in making payments, the seller must give him notice of that default before he can enforce his right to terminate the agreement or recover the goods, and in many cases this right can only be enforced through the courts.

7. *Mistake*

The cases in which mere mistake has any effect upon validity of a contract are comparatively few—fewer probably than in most other systems of law. In the case of a sale, for instance, we do not attempt to make any distinction between a mistake as to quality and a mistake as to substance. A person who has bought a specific piece of plate cannot avoid his bargain because he believed it to be of old workmanship when in truth it was modern, or gold when it was really silver-gilt. It makes no difference even that the seller knew of his mistake, so long as he did nothing to cause or confirm it. If, however, the buyer thought not merely that the thing was different from what it really was, but that the seller was undertaking that it had some quality which it had not, and the seller knew of his mistake, he cannot hold him to his bargain. Of course, if the seller promises an article of a certain kind and supplies one of a different kind, the purchaser need not accept it; but here there is no mistake but a default in performance. The contract holds good, and the purchaser can recover damages for the default. Somewhat similar is the converse case, where a man offers more than he means to offer (as by a mistake in writing figures), and the other party accepts the offer knowing that it has been made by mistake. The courts decided in a series of cases in 1992 and 1993 that if an overpayment of a sum due under a contract is mistakenly made, and the payee was unaware of this at the time, the payee is not bound to repay the excess unless there was something connected with the transaction, either oral or in documentary form, which should have alerted him to the possible overpayment, in which case he is not entitled to keep the overpayment. On the other hand a public authority, such as the Inland Revenue, is under a Common Law duty to repay any sum paid to it without lawful authority.

The most important cases in which the mistake of one party will make a contract void are where there is a mistake as to the whole nature of the transaction (as when a man signs a bill of exchange believing he is signing a guarantee, or that he is signing merely as a witness), and where there is a mistake as to the identity of the other party (as when an order for goods is sent, to which the sender has forged the name of another). Such cases can hardly arise except through fraud; but whereas a fraud in itself does no more than give the person deceived the right to avoid the contract—a right which cannot be exercised against an innocent third person who has acquired ownership under it for value—a mistake of the kind mentioned is held to prevent the formation of any contract at all, so that even innocent third persons can acquire no rights. Thus in the case of the forged order the seller could recover the goods even from an innocent person who had purchased from the forger; if the goods had been obtained by a false representation—say as to the credit or solvency of the buyer—the innocent purchaser from him would have been safe.

A mistake common to both parties as to the existence of what is contracted for—e.g. a sale of a life policy or of an annuity, when the life in question has already ceased—will make the contract void, and what has been paid under it may be recovered. Where there are two things which equally answer the description of the thing contracted for—two ships, for instance, with the same name—and each party is thinking of a different one, it has been held that there is no contract. It is possible, but not clear, that the same would be held when a thing is sufficiently described by the one party, but the other makes a mistake as to what is intended—e.g. at a sale by auction a man through deafness bids for one lot thinking that another is being offered.

8. *Misrepresentation and fraud*

A misrepresentation made by one person to another, with the purpose and effect of inducing him to enter into a contract with the former, will entitle the latter to avoid the contract, if it is a misrepresentation as to some material fact, such as the quality of goods to be sold, or the character or credit of a person to be dealt with. A statement of opinion or intention is not and does not become a misrepresentation because the opinion turns out to be mistaken or the intention is not carried out; but the existence of the opinion or intention is a matter of fact, and a false representation that it exists may well be a material misrepresentation. If a representation is not merely false, but is known to be so to the person who makes it, or is made by him recklessly without knowing or caring whether it be true or false, it is called fraud or deceit. For the purpose of giving a right to avoidance of the contract it makes little difference whether a misrepresentation is innocent or fraudulent, save that it will be harder to resist the inference that a fraudulent misrepresentation was made for the purpose of inducing the contract.

In general there is no duty requiring a party to any intended contract to make a disclosure to the other of material facts which might affect his judgement. But there are special kinds of contract (*uberrimae fidei*)—notably contracts of insurance—in which the facts are usually so much more within the knowledge of one party, that the law imposes on him the duty of disclosure, and gives the other a right to avoidance if the duty is not discharged. In contracts for the sale of land or goods, the vendor is bound to give a good title, subject to such exceptions as may be provided for by the conditions of sale; and the existence of an undisclosed defect in the title may give the purchaser a right to repudiate, though rather as a breach of the seller's duty under the contract than as a failure in a duty antecedent to it. The same is true of the conditions as to merchantable quality and fitness which, in certain circumstances, are implied in a sale of goods. Certain social security benefits paid under the modern welfare state result from contracts which persons are obliged to enter into, as for example where they are bound by law to pay contributions to the National Insurance Fund.

Duress and undue influence have effects similar to that of fraud: the former consists in actual or threatened violence or imprisonment inflicted by the one party on the other or on members of his family, the latter of an unconscientious use of power arising out of confidential relations (like those of parent and child or solicitor and client), or out of special circumstances which put one party in a position of great disadvantage towards the other.

The right to avoid a contract, and even a transaction completed by conveyance, on any of the grounds above mentioned, is subject to the rights acquired by third persons for value and in good faith, and to the possibility that the right of avoidance may be lost by a positive confirmation of the transaction, or by acquiescence in it after the cause which induced it has ceased to operate.

9. *Illegality*

It is obvious that no system of law could enforce a promise to commit acts, such as crimes or even civil wrongs, which are contrary to law. The same is true of contracts for the commission of acts, such as sexual immorality, which the law seeks to discourage, though it does not punish. Contracts of these kinds are said to be void for illegality, and the invalidity extends to the whole contract, including the counter-promise of acts innocent in themselves, such as a promise of payment, for which the illegal or immoral act or the promise of it forms the consideration. But the term 'illegality' as applied to contracts has a wider scope in its application to contracts which the law holds void, not because what is promised is illegal or immoral, but because in some cases it is contrary to the policy of the law that a person should be bound to observe his promise. It is not illegal or immoral for a man to refrain from trading in any part of the United Kingdom or to cease to trade at all; but it is contrary to public policy that he should bind himself to abstain from trading either generally or within limits wider than are reasonable under the circumstances; and a contract in restraint of trade, which cannot be proved to be reasonable in reference both to the interests of the parties to the contract and to the interests of the public, will be held void. It would be an unreasonable restraint if an Oxford grocer, on selling his business, undertook to carry on no similar business within a radius of 150 miles. Similarly it would be an unreasonable restraint if an employee contracted that, should he leave his employer's service, he would never practise the same trade or business. But it has been held not unreasonable for a manufacturer of munitions of war, upon selling his undertaking, to agree not to carry on certain classes of business in any part of the world. It is not illegal or immoral to pay money lost on a wager; but the practice of making wagers is discouraged by statutes which greatly restrict actions in respect of wagering contracts. Second marriages are neither illegal nor immoral; but a promise by a married man, other than one who has actually obtained a decree *nisi* for divorce, or against whom such a decree has been obtained, to marry another if his present marriage should be terminated is void. So again a man may lawfully commit the custody of his children to another; but he cannot, unless he formally gives them in adoption, bind himself not to resume their control or fetter his liberty of deciding as to their religious education.

Where property has been transferred or money paid under an illegal contract, the law will give no assistance to a party who seeks to recover it, except in the case of 'marriage-brokage contracts' (where one person agrees to pay another a sum of money for his services in bringing about a marriage). Bets once paid cannot be got back. But the same rule is not applied where money has been deposited with a stake-holder to abide the result of a wager: the depositor who has lost may reclaim his deposit at any time before it has been paid over to the winner. Nor is the rule applied where the illegal purpose has as yet been in no way carried out (as in the case of a transfer of property with a view to defrauding creditors), or where the party who claims to recover is the less guilty of the two (such as a tenant who has paid 'key-money', the exaction of which is illegal under the Rent Acts, for the lease of a flat). In a case decided in 1978 a woman in England had paid out £9,400 for the purchase of a house in Spain, but had inadvertently failed to obtain the Treasury permission necessary at that time under exchange control legislation to remit money to persons abroad. The vendor had no good title to the house concerned, and thus was guilty of fraud. The court therefore decided that the fact that the plaintiff had not deliberately broken the law was sufficient to allow her to recover the money she had paid.

10. *Limits and extensions of contractual rights and duties*

The rights and duties under a contract are, in the first instance, limited to the parties to it, who have 'privity of contract' with each other. If A promises a sum of money to B, no one but A is liable, and no one but B can claim. Even if the promise is made by A to B that A will pay C, C acquires no rights; the fact that C would benefit if the contract were performed will not alter the situation. But this limited operation of contract may be extended in various ways. We have already seen that a contract made by an agent may place the principal in the same position as if he had himself made the contract. So too rights under a contract, in so far as they are not of too personal a nature, may form the subject of an assignment or trust which will enable the assignee or beneficiary to enforce them. Such rights and the corresponding obligations will also pass upon the death of a contracting party to his representatives. Recently the Law Commission has suggested abolition of the privity of contract rule altogether so that a third party should be able to sue on a contract if that is what the contracting parties intended, but legislation to implement this is still awaited.

A glaring anomaly was corrected in 1957. The House of Lords, by a decision in 1906, pushed the rule of rigid privity of contract to extreme lengths, by holding that if a landlord promises his tenant to repair the house, and for default of repair a visitor to the house is injured, the latter will have no claim against the landlord. But this decision was reversed by the Occupiers' Liability Act 1957, the provision of which has now been replaced by the still stronger Defective Premises Act 1972. The position now is that where a landlord is under an obligation to his tenant to maintain or repair the premises, or else has a right to enter and repair but no obligation to do so, he owes to those whose persons and goods are lawfully on the premises the same duty, in respect of dangers arising out of his failure to fulfil his covenant, as if he were occupier, and the persons or goods were on the premises by his invitation or permission. This duty of care is also owed to all who might reasonably be expected to be affected by defects in the premises, such as passers-by or neighbours.

The benefit and burden of covenants which 'touch and concern' land are in many cases treated as annexed to proprietary interests in the land, and pass or 'run' with them. The application of this principle to the covenants in leases has already been mentioned (p. 95). In the case of sales of land the benefit of the vendor's covenants for title 'runs' with the land purchased. So too the benefit of covenants, and even of less formal agreements, between adjacent owners relating to the erection of buildings or the use of land may pass with the land for the benefit of which they are entered into. The burden of such covenants or agreements will, however, bind a subsequent owner only if the obligation is negative—e.g. a covenant *not to build* a house worth less than £100,000, but not a covenant *to build* a house of that value—and even so it will not bind a purchaser for 'money or money's worth' of a legal estate, unless the covenant was duly registered as a land charge.

The Resale Prices Act 1964 in effect re-establishes the old Common Law rule (which had been altered in 1956) that a restrictive covenant with regard to goods cannot bind a third party as to the price at which he sells those goods, though there is provision for the resale prices of some goods to be exempted from this rule by the court in certain cases. During the past forty years there have been several attempts by the Government, under temporary statutory authority, to curb increases in the price of goods and of wages, by providing, *inter alia*, that a contracting party may safely disregard any term in a contract providing for such an increase, and by prohibiting certain increases. But no formula has yet been found for generally acceptable permanent legislation on the subject.

11. *Negotiable instruments*

Negotiable instruments, which include bills of exchange, cheques, and promissory notes, were transferable by the custom of merchants, and their transferability has long been recognized by our courts. To take the most familiar example, a cheque is an order for payment of money on demand, drawn on a banker, and expressed to be payable either to bearer or to a named person or his order. As between the drawer and the payee it is a promise by the former to pay money to the latter. If it is payable to bearer, the rights of the holder may be transferred by him by merely handing over the cheque. If payable to order, the payee can transfer his rights only by endorsement, i.e. by signing his name on the back. If he so signs without more, the endorsement is said to be in blank, and the cheque becomes payable to bearer. He may, however, make a special endorsement, i.e. order payment to some other named person who must again endorse. The Cheques Act 1992 has provided some greater security to those who draw cheques by giving legal force to the words 'account payee' now commonly written or printed on cheques. Payment may only be made lawfully to the named payee, and the cheque cannot be endorsed over to anyone else.

When a cheque is transferred, whether by delivery or endorsement, it is said to be negotiated, and negotiation is a kind of transfer which differs in important respects from the ordinary assignment of a contractual right. In the first place, any holder of a cheque to bearer—even a thief—can give a good title to one who takes from him for value and in good faith; it passes like money. In the second place, a transfer by endorsement gives a good title to the endorsee who takes in good faith and for value, free from any defences on the ground of fraud, duress, or illegality, which might have been available against the endorser, except that a holder who is shown to have been a party to such fraud, duress, or illegality cannot recover. Further, we may notice that the rule as to consideration is modified in respect of negotiable instruments. A cheque given gratuitously, it is true, creates no rights between the drawer and the payee if the former can prove the absence of consideration. But a subsequent holder who has given value for it is in as good a position as if value had been given by the original payee, and a gratuitous transferee from the holder for value is in an equally good position. It may thus come about that a holder who has given nothing for a cheque can successfully sue a drawer who has received nothing: it is sufficient that once in the cheque's career value has been given. It is presumed in favour of a holder in due course that value has been given; but if once it is shown that the drawing or negotiation has been effected by fraud, duress, or illegality, the burden is shifted on to the shoulders of the holder to prove that subsequently value has in good faith been given.

The late twentieth century has however seen a revolution in accounting and communication, and there must be few businesses still working without computers, while more and more people use plastic credit cards of one kind or another to pay for their purchases. Cash is of course still used for many transactions, and cheques remain commonplace, but the day may not be far off when both become much more rarely used than credit cards. It is no surprise therefore that Parliament is turning its attention towards legislation to combat fraud induced by the new technology, e.g. the Computer Misuse Act 1990 designed to criminalize the unauthorized access to computer systems.

12. *Breach of contract*

Any failure to perform what is promised is a breach of contract, which will give the injured party the right to bring an action in which he will recover damages. In general, damages will be of such amount as to place him, so far as money can do it, in the same position as if the contract had been performed—subject, however, to the rule that damages are not to be given for losses of an extraordinary kind, such as the parties could not be presumed to have contemplated at the time of entering into the contract: e.g. a purchaser of goods who, unknown to the seller, has agreed to sell them again at a large profit, is not entitled, if the seller fails to deliver, to charge him with the loss of profit, but only with the difference between the contract price and the price at which other goods of the same kind might have been bought in the market when the breach occurred. In some cases the damages allowed by law are merely nominal: for instance, for failure to pay a debt at the time agreed, nothing beyond the amount of the debt itself can in most cases be recovered. On the other hand, in the case of breach of promise of marriage, damages used to be given as compensation for injured feelings. In an age of growing sexual equality this was clearly out of line with modern needs, and so breach of promise of marriage was abolished as a cause of action in 1970. More recently, where a surgeon contracted with a married couple in impoverished circumstances to perform a vasectomy on the husband so as to make him irreversibly sterile, substantial damages were awarded against him when the couple later had a healthy daughter, the damages covering the costs of the birth and also of the child's upkeep until her seventeenth birthday.

A contract sometimes provides that a certain sum shall be paid on breach, and rules have been laid down for determining whether such a sum is to be deemed a penalty, i.e. a sum which bears no reference to any loss which may be suffered, recovery of which will be refused, or is liquidated damages, i.e. represents a prospective assessment of the probable loss, and can be recovered. The decision will turn only to a slight extent on the question whether the expression 'penalty' or 'liquidated damages' has been used in the contract. Under the Industrial Relations Act 1971, as subsequently re-enacted, an employee may obtain compensation in proceedings before an industrial tribunal where he has been unfairly dismissed by his employer.

Negative duties under a contract may also be enforced by means of an injunction, an order of the court forbidding the doing of an act. In certain cases a positive duty may be enforced by order for specific performance, a remedy which is almost confined to contracts for the sale or conveyance of interests in land, and for the transfer of other property which is either unique or so rare that damages would be an inadequate remedy. The court has a discretion in granting an injunction and an order for specific performance, and in exercising the discretion will have regard to all the circumstances of the case, and in particular to the conduct of the party asking for it. Non-compliance with an order of either kind may be punished by imprisonment.

In modern business practice it has been common for those who sell or hire out goods to seek to limit or exclude their common law liability for negligence by means of a term in the contract to that effect. This inevitably places a purchaser or hirer at a disadvantage, especially where the party attempting to reduce his future liabilities holds a virtual monopoly in the provision of the goods sought, e.g. a motor-vehicle manufacturer or a service industry. In a number of decisions in this century the courts have nullified many of the intentions behind 'exclusion clauses' in contracts by holding that some act or omission is a *fundamental* breach of the contract not covered by the clause in point. And now, by the Unfair Contract Terms Act 1977, it is provided that liability for negligence in respect of death or personal injuries cannot be excluded at all by contract, and that such liability in respect of other loss or damage can only be excluded or restricted in so far as the term in the contract satisfies the test of reasonableness. In order to satisfy this latter test a term must be fair and reasonable having regard to the circumstances known to the parties at the time when the contract was made.

In a recent case the plaintiff had applied for a building society mortgage, and the society obtained a valuation from surveyors. The valuation report stated that the property needed no essential repairs and was readily saleable, but it also contained a disclaimer of liability for its accuracy. In fact the surveyor had overlooked a serious defect, namely that the chimney breasts in two first-floor rooms had been cut away, and some eighteen months after the plaintiff's purchase the chimneys collapsed, causing extensive damage. The House of Lords held that the disclaimer was ineffective under the 1977 Act because it would not be fair and reasonable to allow a valuer to rely on it to exclude his liability to the mortgagor who was entitled to treat the report as a professional opinion.

13. *The termination of contractual rights and liabilities*

Besides the fact that the rights and duties which arise under a contract come to an end when they are satisfied by performance, we may notice that a contract will often expressly provide that its force shall cease upon the happening of a specified event.

Further, it may appear from the terms of a contract that the parties contemplated the continuance of a state of things as the basis of it, and in such a case the obligations of the contract will cease as from the time when that state of things ceases. Contracts for personal service are thus dependent on the continued life and health of the person who has promised his services, and as a rule on the life of the employer. The principle was pushed to great lengths in the case of contracts for seats to view King Edward VII's Coronation, which was postponed through the King's illness; and its application presented many problems during the wars of 1914–18 and 1939–45, and as a result of the Suez Crisis in 1956.

The failure by one party to perform his obligations under a contract does not necessarily release the other; but it may do so where a condition to this effect is expressed or can be implied in the contract; where the failure amounts to a complete repudiation, or renders it impossible for the other to perform; or where it is so complete as to deprive the other of the whole substantial benefit of the contract.

An impossibility of performance created by a change in the law puts an end to duties under a contract. Other cases in which it is said that impossibility arising after the making of a contract puts an end to it seem to fall under the principle above stated, which applies where the parties have contemplated the continuance of some state of things as the basis of it.

The parties may agree after the making of a contract, and even after its breach, to put an end to their rights and liabilities. Such an agreement is governed by the ordinary principles relating to the formation of contracts. It follows that, where there are outstanding liabilities on both sides, a mutual discharge is good in whatever form it is made because the discharge which each gives is a consideration for the discharge given by the other; where there is a liability on one side only, the other can give up his rights only by deed or in return for some new consideration. If the right which is to be discharged is a right of action for breach of contract, it is said that the consideration must be a performance and not merely a promise, and the right is then said to be discharged by 'accord and satisfaction'. The limits of this rule are obscure, but it seems clear that for the purpose of it the execution of a negotiable instrument is a sufficient performance.

The right of action for breach of contract lapses six years from the breach, in the case of a simple contract; in the case of deeds, and in that of claims for money secured by deed upon land, the period of limitation is twelve years. The right of action for a debt may be kept alive or revived by a part payment or payment of interest, or by a written promise of payment or acknowledgement signed by the debtor. The period then begins to run afresh from the date of the payment or writing, provided that the payment or acknowledgement was made before the normal limitation period had expired. But it is impossible to reopen an expired limitation period by acknowledgement or part payment.

7 Torts

1. *The liability for tort*

The account of the law of contract given in the last chapter shows that English law (unlike Roman law) has developed a set of comprehensive rules relating to the formation, validity, and effect of contracts, and has laid comparatively little stress on the differences arising between various kinds of contracts from the nature of their subject-matter. It was for a long time doubtful whether any such statement could be made as to liability for wrongs which are independent of breach of contract and trust, i.e. for tort. Until the latter part of the nineteenth century the prevalent opinion was that the law only recognized liability for a number of specific torts, and that no act entailed liability for tort unless it fell under some one or other of them. But at the present day the prevalent opinion is that the law recognizes the general principle that any harm to a person caused intentionally or negligently creates a liability in tort, unless the person causing the harm has some just cause or excuse for his act or omission. It is true that the largest part of the detailed rules of the law of tort has grown up round the conditions laid down by the courts as to the circumstances in which specific torts can be committed. At the same time it must not be forgotten that for centuries the courts, as occasion arose, have never hesitated to create new torts. Thus the modern tort of deceit emerged at the end of the eighteenth century; and the modern tort of negligence, i.e. the failure to perform a legal duty to the damage of the plaintiff, emerged in the earlier half of the nineteenth century.

It was inevitable that, as rules as to many different torts old and new accumulated, some general principles of liability should emerge, with the result that it is now possible to say that the infliction of unjustifiable harm creates a liability in tort. Today, therefore, it is in many cases important to consider, not so much whether any given acts falls under some specific head of tort, as whether, if one person has harmed another, he has some just cause or excuse for his act. Whether or not he has some just cause or excuse is a question which depends very largely upon the general conditions in which the law will impose a liability for tort. The House of Lords affirmed in 1994 that a plaintiff who has available to him remedies in both contract and tort is free to choose that which is most advantageous to him unless the contract precludes him from doing so.

2. *General conditions of liability*

(*a*) *Intention.* The consequences of an act may be said to be intended when the person acting contemplates that they will necessarily or probably follow from it, whether that consequence be desired for its own sake or not. It is said that a man is presumed to intend the probable consequences of his acts, but failure to anticipate probable consequences is really negligence rather than intention, and if the saying is more than a rule of evidence for ascertaining intention, it only means that for some purposes negligence, no less than intention, creates liability. Although some torts clearly cannot be committed unintention-ally (e.g. fraud), it is a general condition of liability that other wrongful acts will become torts if intentionally committed.

(*b*) *Motive and malice.* The motive with which an act is done is for the most part immaterial. A lawful act does not become unlawful because it is done with a bad motive, such as ill-will; nor is an unlawful act excused because it is done with the best of motives. There are, however, some kinds of tort in which malice forms, or appears to form, an essential ingredient.

The right enjoyed by every citizen of prosecuting criminals is given for the purpose of vindicating law and justice, and a prosecutor who uses his right for the purpose of ill-will or extortion, or for any other than the proper purpose, will (if certain other conditions are also present) incur liability for malicious prosecution.

In claims for defamation the plaintiff alleges that the words spoken or written were published 'maliciously', but this phrase has nothing to do with motive, and merely denies by anticipation the existence of any ground of defence. On the other hand, when a defence of privilege is raised, and this is answered by an allegation of 'express (or actual) malice', the answer amounts to saying that the defendant has used his privilege for some purpose other than that for which the law allows it.

(*c*) *Negligence.* Negligence which harms another unjustifiably is not only a tort in itself, it is also a condition of liability for tort. From this point of view it is, like intention, a mental state. It has been defined as 'omitting to do something which a reasonable man would do, or the doing of something which a reasonable man would not do'; more shortly, one may say that it is a failure to use proper care in one's conduct. Negligence will in general involve liability for damage caused by it; but, before we can say that there has been negligence of which the law will take account, one must make sure that there is a legally recognized duty to take care. It was held by the House of Lords in 1963 that a person may, quite apart from contract, be under a duty to take care that his statements are true where he gives information or advice in circumstances which establish a relationship creating a duty not only to be honest but also to be careful. Thus accountants who negligently prepare a falsely optimistic statement of the accounts of a company for inclusion in the company's prospectus would be liable to any investor who suffers financial loss as a result of buying the company's shares in reliance upon the stated accounts. But they would not be so liable to another company which was known to be likely to make a take-over bid; and an insurance company gratuitously and negligently giving wrong information to one of its policy-holders on the financial stability of an associated company, in which the policy-holder wished to invest, was held not to be under such a duty of care, because it did not hold itself out in business to give such advice. Again, an owner of land is under no duty to take care that the growth of thistles upon it shall not cause damage to his neighbours. In an action brought against the Chief Constable of a police force on behalf of the estate of the last victim of the so-called 'Yorkshire Ripper' murderer it was held that the police owe no duty of care to one member of the public in respect of an attack on her perpetrated by another, and so the defendant could not be found negligent in failing to apprehend the murderer before he struck.

The House of Lords also held in 1969 that a barrister or solicitor normally owes his client a duty of care, any breach of which will render him liable to his client, except where he is acting as an advocate, when he will not be liable for negligence in his conduct of a case. The reason for this exception is that an advocate owes his main duty to the court, so that there is a general public interest in his complete freedom in the conduct of a trial; and it follows that the advocate's immunity from liability for professional negligence extends to any pre-trial work which is intimately connected with the conduct of the case in court. It may also be noted that to allow an action for negligence to be brought against an advocate by his client would inevitably lead to an undesirable retrial of the merits of the original case. Nevertheless in the 1980s the Law Society set up a Solicitors Complaints Bureau to consider complaints about poor service given to clients by solicitors, and make awards of compensation against them where appropriate; and a Review Body set up by the Bar Council recommended in 1994 that there should be a similar Barristers Complaints Bureau. This is now expected to come into being by January 1996. Overall consideration of complaints about the way in which the professional bodies have dealt with complaints against solicitors and barristers rests with the Legal Services Ombudsman, set up by the Courts and Legal Services Act 1990, who may also recommend payments of compensation. Such recommendations, though strictly not en-forceable, are in practice complied with.

The circumstances in which purely economic or financial loss will give rise to legal liability for negligence are limited. The House of Lords held in 1990 that liability for such loss only exists where the damage or harm to the plaintiff was reasonably foreseeable by the defendant, the relationship between the two parties was sufficiently proximate to give rise to a duty, and it is just and reasonable to impose such a duty. Thus, where a home owner suffered financial loss because he had to remedy a dangerous defect to his house he was unsuccessful in suing the District Council which had negligently failed, in the course of its statutory building control functions, to ensure that the building was designed and erected in compliance with the applicable building regulations. The owner would be able to recover his loss only from the builder by suing for breach of contract, or else by a claim under an insurance policy. On the other hand it was held in 1994 that an employer owes a duty to take reasonable care in the preparation of a reference for a former employee, and will be liable to the former employee if he suffers loss as a result of inaccuracy in the reference caused by negligence.

It would be impossible to enumerate all the occasions on which a duty to take care arises, nor has the law exhaustively defined them; but we may notice the duty of persons who use vehicles upon the highway; the duty of owners of premises to prevent them from being a source of danger to those upon the highway, or to neighbours, or to persons who resort to them as lawful visitors; the duty of persons who deliver goods to others to take care that they are free from danger, or in some circumstances to give warning of any known defect; the duty of a farmer who sprays his rape crop with insecticide to avoid spraying at a time when the insecticide would be likely to kill or harm his neighbour's bees which he knows are attracted by the rape flowers. The extent and degree of care necessary will vary according to the circumstances, but there is no sharp line of division such as is suggested by the use of such terms as 'gross' or 'slight' negligence.

Particular difficulties arise where a plaintiff claims to have suffered nervous shock as a result of negligence. The court will only allow his claim where there is a relationship of proximity

between plaintiff and defendant, and it is also reasonably foreseeable that some form of psychiatric illness might occur. The
South Yorkshire Police had been responsible for crowd control
at the Hillsborough Stadium, Sheffield on the day in 1989 when
95 people were killed and over 400 injured after overcrowding
and subsequent crowd panic. Actions by relatives of those in the
crowd against the Chief Constable for nervous shock caused by
watching the disaster on live television were rejected by the
House of Lords because the plaintiffs had not been within sight
or hearing of what happened to those they loved.

The Unfair Contract Terms Act 1977, already referred to in
the last chapter, provides that liability for negligence in respect
of death or personal injuries cannot be excluded at all either by
contract or by any non-contractual notice, and that such liability
in respect of other loss or damage can only be excluded or
restricted in so far as the term or notice satisfies the reasonableness test already mentioned above (p. 148). The duty of care
owed by occupiers of premises to lawful visitors was introduced
(altering the previous law on this point which had been rather
out of line with other common law rules) by the Occupiers'
Liability Act 1957; and this duty has in effect been extended to
many trespassers by the Occupiers' Liability Act 1984. The 1984
Act imposes a duty on an occupier to take such care as is
reasonable in all the circumstances of the case to see that
uninvited entrants do not suffer injury by reason of any risk of
which he is aware or has reasonable grounds to believe exists.

It may be that, though B has through his negligence harmed
A, yet the proximate cause of the harm may have been the
'contributory negligence' of A. The Law Reform (Contributory
Negligence) Act 1945 pursues the path of sensible apportionment
of damages, by providing that 'where any person suffers damage
as the result partly of his own fault and partly of the fault of any
other person, a claim in respect of that damage shall not be
defeated by reason of the fault of the person suffering the
damage, but the damages recoverable in respect thereof shall be
reduced to such extent as the Court thinks just and equitable
having regard to the claimant's share in the responsibility for the

damage'. (For the position under the Maritime Conventions Act 1911, see p. 45.) In 1994 the Law Commission recommended that a similar apportionment of damages should be made in cases of breach of contract where the plaintiff has contributed to his loss, and it remains to be seen if this is implemented. More radically, serious consideration is currently being given to a new way of dealing with the results of motor accidents, which have become such a prevalent part of modern life. It may well be that within a few years the law of negligence will, for less serious road accidents, be replaced by a no-fault compensation scheme financed by private insurance, probably modelled on the scheme now operating in New Zealand.

(*d*) *Liability independent of intention or negligence.* In some exceptional circumstances a person may incur liability for damage which is not intentionally caused by him nor due to any negligence on his part. Thus a person who creates a dangerous state of things upon his land, as by the construction of a reservoir, will be liable for damage resulting to others from water if, for instance, the reservoir bursts, although he has used every precaution, unless the accident is due to the act of a stranger or to some natural event of extraordinary violence (an 'act of God'), such as a flood caused by exceptional rainfall. The person who keeps a wild animal of a dangerous species, or even a domestic animal which is known to him to have dangerous characteristics—for instance, a dog which he knows to have bitten human beings—will be liable for damage done by it, whatever care he may have used to keep it safely. The keeping of a dangerous wild animal, unless under a local authority licence, or in a zoological garden, circus, or licensed pet shop, is made a crime by the Dangerous Wild Animals Act 1976, as is the keeping of dogs bred for fighting, except under strict conditions, by the Dangerous Dogs Act 1991. Further, a statutory strict liability has been imposed on the owner of a dog for damage done by it to livestock, even if he had no knowledge of its propensity to do such damage; and a man is strictly liable for damage done to crops by his horses and cattle straying from his land. He is also liable if his acts interfere with another's possession of, or right to possess, his land or chattels—if, for instance, he enters the plaintiff's land, or carries off his goods, or uses his goods in a manner which is inconsistent with the plaintiff's right to possess them. Conduct of the type last named with regard to goods constitutes the tort of conversion, which bears with especial harshness on someone who has, in all good faith, bought goods from one who had no title to them.

An important new area of strict liability is introduced by the Consumer Protection Act 1987, under which the manufacturers of a wide range of consumer products are liable for damage caused by defects in such products regardless of fault.

(*e*) *Damage and damages*. In some cases the mere infringement of a right is itself a cause of action, though there may have been no pecuniary loss and not even any appreciable harm done, as in the case of trespass to land or goods. Here, if no actual damage is proved, and there are no circumstances of aggravation, such as insulting conduct, only nominal damages are recoverable. In the bulk of cases damages will be computed on the basis of the actual damage suffered, worked out by a jury, which is now in practice found only in cases of defamation and fraud, or more commonly by a judge, who decides issues of law and fact alike. In some cases in which the conduct of the defendant may be regarded as exceptionally bad, this may be taken notice of by the award of heavy damages, technically known as exemplary. Where the continuance or repetition of a tort is threatened, the judge may grant an injunction, which may take an affirmative or 'mandatory' form. So if B has actually built a wall which deprives A's premises of 'ancient lights', B will be ordered to pull the wall down. In recent years injunctions have also been granted to prevent former members of the security service MI5 from disclosing information gained in the course of their service. The injunction is particularly common in the tort of nuisance, in which an award of damages is unlikely to be an adequate remedy. Somewhat different are the cases of injurious acts, such as libel or malicious prosecution, which are actionable without proof of any pecuniary loss, and for which heavy damages may be given, having regard not only to any pecuniary loss, but to the injured feelings of the plaintiff and the improper conduct of the defendant. Again, in the majority of cases of slander, no action lies, unless 'special damage', in the sense of some pecuniary loss, is proved; but the damages recoverable are not limited to the amount of such 'special damage'. Lastly, in the case of a number of torts (e.g. deceit), proof of actual damage is both a condition of actionability and the measure of the damages recoverable. It was laid down by the House of Lords in a case of 1956 that in assessing damages for loss of earnings the court should take into account the amount of tax the plaintiff would have had to pay, had the injury not been suffered, and deduct this for the purposes of the award.

3. *Termination of liability*

(*a*) *Death of either party*. This resolves itself into two distinct questions.

(i) If A is killed by an act of B for which, had he lived, he could have sued B, can anyone else recover damages from B in respect of his death? The general rule is that the death of a human being gives no cause of action to a survivor. But this is subject to an important series of statutory exceptions, constituted by the Fatal Accidents Act 1976 (as amended by the Administration of Justice Act 1982), and the Carriage by Air Act 1961 (as amended by the Carriage by Air and Road Act 1979). These enable certain near relatives, who were dependants of the deceased, to recover damages in respect of any injury suffered by them on account of the death. A person who has lived with the deceased as husband or wife for at least two years immediately before the deceased's death may also so recover, even though they were not actually married. The sum awarded is a matter of pure arithmetic; the dependants are bringing their own action, and in no sense succeeding to that of the deceased.

(ii) If a person against whom a tort has been committed dies, can his executor succeed to his cause of action in respect of it, and can the executor of a deceased tortfeasor be sued for the tort? The law is contained in the Law Reform (Miscellaneous Provisions) Act 1934, as amended. All causes of action, subsisting in or vested in any person, survive against or for the benefit of his estate, except actions for defamation, and for claims for damages for bereavement or for loss of income after death. But in actions brought under this Act exemplary damages are recoverable only against, and not by, an executor, whose claim is confined to damages which represent, so far as possible, the pecuniary loss suffered. The executor is suing or being sued as representative of the deceased, not as a 'dependant' on his own account; if he is also a dependant, any sum recovered by him under the Act of 1934 must go in reduction of the amount recoverable by him under the other Acts, whose provisions are described in dealing with question (i).

(*b*) *Limitation of actions.* In general an action in tort must be begun within six years of the commission of the tort, subject to the following exceptions:

Actions under the Fatal Accidents Act 1976 must be begun within three years of either the death of the deceased person or the date of knowledge of the death by the person for whose benefit the action is brought, whichever is the later, unless the action is one for which a period of limitation is prescribed by some other Act. By the Maritime Conventions Act 1911, actions upon claims in respect of damage to a vessel or her cargo, or in respect of loss of life or personal injuries suffered by any person on board a vessel, must normally be begun within two years. By the Limitation Act 1980 actions for personal injuries through negligence, nuisance, or breach of duty must be begun within three years, and this period applies to every defendant, including 'public authorities', who were formerly in a privileged position as defendants. Where, however, the plaintiff is unaware of the cause of action until after the three-year period has run (as where a miner contracts pneumoconiosis several years after his exposure to silica dust started as a result of his employers' breach of duty), the Limitation Act permits him to start proceedings within three years of the date that he was, or reasonably ought to have been, aware of the facts. Furthermore, in respect of an action either under the Fatal Accidents Act or for personal injuries, the court has the power to override the normal limitation period if it appears to the court that it would be equitable to allow an action to proceed. There is also, under the Administration of Justice Act 1982, a general power for the court to award provisional damages where there is a chance that an injured person may later develop a serious disease or suffer serious deterioration in his physical or mental condition. Claims to the possession of land must be brought within twelve years after the wrongdoer, or those under whom he claims, first took possession; but if the person in possession gives a written acknowledgement of the claimant's title before the period has elapsed, the period begins to run again.

The Latent Damage Act 1986 makes special provision for cases where the plaintiff is unaware of a cause of action for damages for negligence, other than for personal injuries. Such an action must be begun within six years of the cause of action occurring or within three years of the earliest date on which the plaintiff has both the knowledge required for bringing an action and a right to bring it, whichever is the later. And the limitation period for beginning actions for libel or slander was reduced from six to three years by the Administration of Justice Act 1985.

4. *Specific torts*

(*a*) *Wrongs to personal safety and liberty.* 'The least touching of a man in anger is a battery', and any direct application of force to a man's person, whether intentional or negligent, is an actionable wrong. The attempt and even the threat of immediate violence where there is something more than mere threatening language, and there is present power and intention to do violence—aiming a gun, for instance, or shaking one's fist in a man's face—is also actionable, and is known as an assault, a term which, in its strict legal sense, is distinguished from a battery.

Further, any intentional or negligent doing of actual harm to a man's person, though it may be indirect and not amount to a battery, is an actionable wrong, as where injury is done by placing an obstruction on a highway, or where a medical man does harm through want of care—care including the use of such skill as belongs to his profession. Where illness is caused by apprehension of harm—e.g. where a person is nearly but not quite run into by a negligent driver—damages may be recovered in respect of the illness, though not for the mere mental distress. Where an injury has shortened a person's normal expectation of life he was formerly able to recover moderate damages. The Administration of Justice Act 1982 abolished this direct cause of action, though in awarding damages for pain and suffering the court may still take into account any suffering caused by an awareness that expectation of life has been reduced. The Court of Appeal has recently granted an injunction to restrain a defendant from harassing, pestering, or communicating with a woman by any means, including telephone calls made to her at her parents' home.

'Any restraint of the liberty of a free man is an imprisonment, although he be not within the walls of any common prison', and where such imprisonment is not legally justified it amounts to the wrong of false imprisonment. The restraint must, however, be complete. There is no imprisonment if a person is prevented from going in one or more of several directions in which he has a right to go, so long as it is left open to him to go with reasonable safety in some other direction. Not only confinement or restraint by physical force, but the show of a pretended authority to arrest, if it is complied with, amounts to an imprisonment.

Interferences with a man's person or liberty are of course justified on many grounds. Parental powers of chastisement and coercion, the lawful punishment of criminals, the restraint of persons of unsound mind, are familiar instances. We may note also that it is the right even of a private person to arrest without a warrant someone suspected of being in the act of committing, or having actually committed, one of the more serious crimes;

but the right is exercised at some risk, for if the prisoner's guilt cannot be proved, the person who arrests him can justify himself only by showing both that he had reasonable grounds of suspicion and that the offence was actually committed by someone. A constable who makes an arrest in the like circumstances is justified by merely showing reasonable grounds of suspicion, and in other respects has considerably larger powers of arrest.

Consent to an act (e.g. the voluntary undergoing of surgical treatment, provided it is carried out with proper care and skill) and the voluntary incurring of risk, as in the case of those who engage in a lawful game, provide a defence to most claims in tort. This is known as the principle of *volenti non fit injuria*. The defence is, however, often difficult to prove, as the defendant must establish that the plaintiff had a *full* knowledge and acceptance of risk. Nevertheless the principle operated to deprive of any remedy a shopkeeper through whose open door had strayed an ox, which was being driven along the road. More obviously, a plaintiff who had willingly been a passenger in a light aircraft flown by a pilot he knew to be very drunk was also denied any remedy for injury caused when the pilot crashed the aeroplane. The defence must be distinguished from that of contributory negligence, which admits a prima facie liability. To an action based on the breach of a statutory obligation the latter may be, but the former is not, a valid defence.

(*b*) *Defamation*. This tort is divided into libel and slander. Slander consists of spoken words, libel of some reproduction in permanent form, such as writing. But reproduction in a permanent form is deemed, by the Defamation Act 1952, to include broadcasting for general reception by means of wireless telegraphy, including television, and, since the Theatres Act 1968, the use of words, pictures, visual images, gestures, etc., in the public performance of a play. A representation is defamatory either if it is made in respect of a man's personal character and is calculated to 'injure him in the estimation of right-thinking persons', or if it is calculated to disparage him in any office, profession, calling, trade or business carried on by him.

Publication of a libel or slander consists in communicating it to any third person. In this connection the doctrine that for some purposes 'husband and wife are one person' has been so applied that, while a communication to the wife of the person whose reputation is attacked is a publication, communication to one's own wife is no publication. A publication may be made not only intentionally but negligently, as by putting a book into circulation without taking care to make sure that it contains nothing libellous.

The chief importance of the distinction between libel and slander lies in the rule that, while a libel is actionable without any proof of 'special damage', this is true of only a limited class of imputations made by way of slander, among which imputations of the commission of a criminal offence, of a woman's unchastity, and those calculated to disparage a man in his office or profession are the most important. Special damage means some loss which is pecuniary, or at any rate capable of being estimated in money, such as the loss of custom, or even loss of the hospitality (though not the society) of one's friends.

The proof of the substantial truth of a defamatory statement is a complete defence to any civil action (but not to a criminal prosecution, see p. 186) brought in respect of it, and is known as 'justification'. This defence is, however, dangerous, for it is equivalent to a repetition of the libel, and its failure will incline a jury to give heavier damages. But the Defamation Act 1952 relieves a defendant to the extent that, if the statement contains two or more distinct charges against the plaintiff, the defence will not fail by reason only that the truth of every charge is not proved, if the words not proved to be true do not materially injure the plaintiff's reputation having regard to the truth of the remaining charges.

In particular circumstances a person is allowed with greater or less impunity to make defamatory statements, so as to incur no liability even if the statement is untrue. A defence founded on such a right is called the defence of privilege. Such privilege arises in numerous circumstances: the proceedings in Parliament; statements made in the course of judicial proceedings by judges, advocates, parties, and witnesses; communications made in private life in the furtherance of some recognized duty or interests—e.g. confidential communications by a former to an intending employer with regard to the character of the employee are all privileged. In some cases the privilege is *absolute*, i.e. it is not lost even if it is shown that the statement was made with knowledge of its falsity, or for mere purposes of ill-will; this is true of the privilege given to statements made in Parliament or in a court of law. In other cases, especially where the privilege exists in private relations, it is said to be *qualified*, and is lost if the statement is shown to have been made with 'actual malice', i.e. with knowledge of its falsehood, or from ill-will, or for any purpose not justified by the circumstances of the privilege. Although corporate bodies may normally sue in defamation in the same way as natural persons, central and local government authorities may not because the House of Lords in 1993 held that to allow them to do so would be against the public interest in placing an undesirable fetter on the freedom of speech: it is of the highest importance that a democratically elected governmental body should be open to uninhibited public criticism.

Disparaging statements made by way of fair comment or criticism on matters of public interest, e.g. the conduct of men in public positions, or published works of art or literature, also enjoy immunity. The defence of fair comment will not cover misstatements of fact, but it will not fail by reason only that the truth of every allegation of fact is not proved, if the expression of opinion is fair comment, having regard to such of the facts alleged or referred to in the words complained of as are proved. The relation of fair comment to privilege is a matter of great difficulty. It is probably safe to say that a criticism actuated by improper motives cannot be a fair comment, even though the same criticism might have been fairly made by a person who had no such motive. But while a successful plea of qualified privilege throws on to the plaintiff the burden of proving malice, in a case in which fair comment is pleaded it is for the defendant, who has made it, to prove that it is fair, not for the plaintiff, against whom it has been made, to prove it unfair.

The Act of 1952 introduced a new defence in cases of 'unintentional defamation'. If the person who has published a statement which annoys another person claims that the publication was made innocently in relation to that person, he may offer to make amends, by way of a suitable apology and financial recompense. The acceptance of his offer precludes any action in respect of the statement; while if the offer is not accepted, proof of its promptitude, and of the absence of intention to injure the plaintiff, will in general operate as a defence, subject to certain conditions laid down in the Act. It is expected that Parliament will shortly vary this provision to enable a defendant to make an offer of amends, but allow the judge to fix the sum to be paid. Apart from the Act, there are certain cases of statements in newspapers in which an apology coupled with a payment of damages into court may be pleaded as a defence or by way of mitigation of damages.

Statements (whether made in writing or otherwise) which are not attacks on a man's character or credit or competence, but which cause damage, e.g. by casting doubts on his title to property, or disparaging the quality of his goods, are not defamatory. Such statements, however, are actionable if they are shown to be false, and to have been made with malice. It is not necessary to prove actual damage, if the statements are calculated to cause pecuniary damage to the plaintiff in respect of his office or profession, or are calculated to cause any other pecuniary damage and are published in writing or other permanent form.

English law does not yet make any specific provision for a right to privacy, but there have been popular fears that the media have on occasions been too intrusive in reporting certain issues. Consultation is currently taking place which may in due course result in legislation establishing a new remedy for infringement of privacy causing substantial distress, but with such defences as absolute or qualified privilege, lawful authority, and public interest.

(c) *Abuse of legal proceedings*. A person may recover damages for malicious prosecution if he can show:

(1) that the defendant instituted against him criminal proceedings of such a kind as to be discreditable to his reputation or to involve possible imprisonment

(2) that the proceedings have resulted in his acquittal, or at least have terminated in his favour by being discontinued

(3) that the proceedings were taken without reasonable and probable cause and

(4) that the proceedings were taken maliciously, i.e. from ill-will or any motive other than a desire to secure the ends of justice.

A somewhat similar liability is incurred by persons who maliciously institute bankruptcy proceedings against a man (or winding-up proceedings against a company), but it is not actionable to institute an ordinary civil action, however maliciously and unreasonably.

(*d*) *Interference with family and contractual relations, business and employment.* An old rule of law recognized that the master had an interest in the services of his servant, for which he was entitled to legal protection against third persons. He was entitled, for instance, to recover damages against a person who wrongfully harmed the servant. However the old actions for enticement, seduction, and for harbouring a wife or child were abolished by the Law Reform (Miscellaneous Provisions) Act 1970; and similar actions in respect of servants, and for loss of the services of a wife, child, or servant, were abolished by the Administration of Justice Act 1982. Nowadays the action for loss of service is superseded by the wider modern rule that it is an actionable wrong for a third person to cause damage by knowingly interfering with contractual relations. It is said that there may be some just cause or excuse for such interference or inducement to break a contract, but it is clear that the motive of self-interest in a trader, who induces the employee of a rival to change masters, is no such cause or excuse. It is difficult to justify the complete exemption from liability for inducement of breach of contract of employment which was given by the Trade Disputes Act 1906, and reinforced by the Trade Disputes Act 1965 and the Trade Union and Labour Relations Act 1974, in the cases where such a breach is induced 'in contemplation or furtherance of a trade dispute'. However, under the Employment Act 1982, this exemption has been substantially reduced, and a trade union may now be sued, and its funds put directly at risk, for unlawful action for which it is legally responsible. The Trade Union Act 1984 now provides also that a union may be liable in tort if it induces a person to break his contract of employment or a commercial contract, or if it interferes with the performance of such contracts, unless such action has been supported by a previous ballot of the members of the union.

Where, without any breach of contract, damage is done to a man's business through interference which consists of acts criminal or wrongful in themselves—for instance, by using violence to his customers—there is no doubt that an action will lie. The same is true where the damage is caused to a trader by a rival who puts goods on the market so got up as to mislead purchasers into thinking that they are purchasing the goods of the former.

Further, an interference with trade or employment, with intent to injure, by persons acting in combination, which causes damage, is an actionable conspiracy at common law, though the interference is carried out by means of acts which in themselves are not unlawful. But if the acts are not in themselves unlawful and are done, not with intent to injure, but only with the intent of furthering the trade interests of the actors, they give rise to no cause of action. A mercantile combination which sought to crush its rivals by underselling them, by offering special advantages to persons who dealt exclusively with members of the combination, and by refusing to employ agents who acted for the rivals, was held to be justified on the ground of furtherance of legitimate trade interests. A similar principle might perhaps justify a spontaneous strike or combination of workmen, even though a trade union cannot now lawfully call a strike without first balloting its members and obtaining a majority vote in favour of the strike.

(e) *Fraud.* Fraud or deceit has already been dealt with as a matter vitiating a contract, and it has the same characteristics when considered as a tort. A person who sues for damage caused by fraud must show that he has suffered damage by acting on a representation made with the intention that he should act on it; that the representation made was false and that it was false to the knowledge of the person making it, or at least was made recklessly without any belief in its truth. The representation need not have been made directly to the person who acts on it, but it must have been made with the intention that it should reach him and that he should act on it.

(*f*) *Torts in respect of property*. Trespass to property consists of any interference with property which is in the possession of another: entry upon land, causing missiles to fall upon it, posting bills on a fence (without the owner's consent), touching or damaging or removing goods, are all acts which amount to trespass. Even an entry on land below the surface, e.g. by mining, is a trespass; but though the ownership of land carries with it a right to restrain encroachments on the space above it, it is not clear that at Common Law passing through the upper air is a trespass with regard to the land below. The Civil Aviation Act 1949 provides that no action shall lie for trespass or nuisance by reason only of the flight of aircraft over property at a height which, having regard to wind, weather, and other circumstances, is reasonable; but, if material damage to person or property is caused by aircraft, damages can be recovered from the owner of the aircraft without proof of negligence or intention, except when the damage was contributed to or caused by the sufferer. If the damage is caused solely by the wrongful act of a person other than the owner or his employees, the owner can recover the amount of the damage from that person.

Trespass is primarily an interference with possession. On the one hand a person in possession of property, whether land or goods, is entitled to resist and to sue any person who interferes with his possession and cannot show a better right to the possession. On the other hand a person who is not in possession and has no present right to the possession—a reversioner of land, an owner of goods who has bound himself by agreement to leave the possession in the hands of another who has hired them for a definite time—cannot complain of a trespass as such, though he may be allowed to sue in a special form of action if he can show that his reversionary interest is damaged. The distinction is important inasmuch as damage is not a condition of bringing an action of trespass. But a person who, though not in actual possession, is entitled to resume immediate possession, e.g. a gratuitous lender of goods, the landlord of a tenant at will, is equally entitled with the actual possessor to sue third persons for trespass.

An act which would otherwise be trespass may be justified if it is done by the consent of the owner, or in the exercise of a public or private right over the land. In the former case, a person who persists in remaining on another's premises when the owner's consent is withdrawn becomes a trespasser; unless he obtained the consent under a binding agreement, as by paying for a ticket, in which case the owner, arbitrarily ejecting him, both breaks the contract and commits a trespass against his person. A right over land must not be used for other purposes than those for which the right exists: a man will be a trespasser on a public footpath if he goes there for the purpose of spying on the owner's adjacent premises or disturbing his game. An owner does not commit a trespass by taking his property from one who is wrongfully in possession of it, but the forcible retaking of land (but not of goods) is a criminal offence.

Not only is it a trespass to deprive an owner of any property of which he is in possession, or even to retain possession of land against the person entitled to it, but in the case of land it constitutes the wrong of dispossession, and in the case of goods is one of the forms of the tort known as conversion.

An owner wrongfully deprived or kept out of possession of land may bring an action to recover the land (sometimes called the action of ejectment), in which he will obtain an order for the restitution of the land itself, as well as damages representing the value of the land for the time during which the wrongful possession has continued.

By conversion of goods is meant any act in relation to goods which amounts to an exercise of dominion over them, inconsistent with the owner's right of property. It does not include mere acts of damage, or even an asportation which does not amount to a denial of the owner's right of property; but it does include such acts as taking possession, refusing to give up on demand, disposing of the goods to a third person, or destroying them. A person who has converted the goods of another will be ordered to restore them, if they are still in his possession, otherwise to pay their value, and in any case to pay damages for the detention. The old tort of detinue (detention of goods short of conversion) was abolished by the Torts (Interference with Goods) Act 1977, and replaced by the statutory tort of 'wrongful interference' with goods.

Though dispossession and conversion are regarded primarily as wrongs done to the owner, yet on the one hand a person who has not a present right to possession—e.g. a person whose estate in land is not a present but a future interest—is not entitled to sue for these wrongs; and on the other hand a man may have obtained possession from another in such a way that, though the latter is not the owner, the former will not be entitled to dispute his right. Thus a jeweller, to whom a chimney-sweep had handed for examination a jewel which he had found, was held liable to restore it to him, though it was obvious that the boy was not the owner.

Ignorance of another's rights is no defence to claims for trespass, dispossession, conversion, or wrongful interference with goods. A man who innocently buys goods from a thief and sells them again must pay their value to the owner.

A private nuisance is an act which, without being trespass, interferes with a person in the enjoyment of his own land or premises, or of some right which he has over the land or premises of another. Thus it is a nuisance, on the one hand, to interfere with the comfort of a dwellinghouse by the persistent production of noise, fumes, or smells, to cause crowds to assemble so as to prevent access to a house or place of business, to divert or pollute the flow of water in a natural stream to which every owner of land abutting on it is entitled, or to display signs in the window of a nearby sex shop indicating that explicit sex acts and uncensored adult videos can be seen inside, and that similar material is for sale; on the other, to interfere with rights of light for windows or private rights of way, or rights of common. It should be noticed that a man has no right of light for his windows unless such a right has been acquired by grant or by long enjoyment; and therefore, in the absence of such a right, it is lawful to cut off light coming to a neighbour's window, by putting structures or buildings on one's own land. Such development of land is, however, subject to the various controls imposed by public authorities under planning law, which is too specialized a subject for the purpose of this book.

A man has a right to have his land in its natural state supported by his neighbour's land, but if he erects buildings which need a greater degree of support he can only acquire a right to it by grant or length of enjoyment. The withdrawal of a right of support, whether natural or acquired, is a nuisance. It is also a nuisance to allow the branches of one's trees to grow so as to overhang one's neighbour's land.

A person who suffers from a nuisance may abate it, i.e. remove it, even without giving notice, if he can do so without going on to another's land, e.g. by cutting overhanging branches; he may even, in case of emergency, enter to abate without notice, but in most cases where entry is made notice should be given.

If an action for nuisance is brought, not only will damages be given, but the court may, and commonly does, grant an injunction forbidding its continuance and even ordering an offending structure to be pulled down. But the granting of an injunction remains a matter solely within the discretion of the court, as was well illustrated by a case decided in 1977. The use of a particular village cricket ground by a cricket club was held by the Court of Appeal to have caused nuisance to those neighbours whose houses had been hit, or whose gardens had been fallen into, by occasional balls struck over the boundary. Damages were awarded, but an injunction against the playing of cricket on the ground was refused, as this would have deprived the local inhabitants of the spectacle of village cricket which had been enjoyed by the community for over seventy years.

A public nuisance is an unlawful act or omission which causes annoyance to the public generally, such as obstructing a highway, or (where there is a duty to repair) failing to repair it, or allowing rubbish and filth to be deposited on one's land to the annoyance of the neighbourhood. For a public nuisance no individual can sue unless he suffers damage peculiar to himself, as by breaking his leg through falling into a hole in the road. A public nuisance is, however, punishable in criminal law, and the Attorney-General may also take civil proceedings to obtain an injunction forbidding its continuance. Local authorities also have power to take proceedings to put a stop to public nuisances. A private person may remove an obstruction on a public way, but he may not repair a public way or bridge.

8 Crimes

1. *Sources of criminal law*

The greater part of our criminal law is now statutory. Much old common law has been codified, and Parliament continually adds new crimes. In addition to the enactment of codes to cover specific areas of crime, the Law Commission in 1989 and 1992 published draft codes for the major portion of the whole range of English criminal law, and in 1993 a comprehensive Bill to codify the whole of the law relating to non-fatal offences against the person. It remains to be seen whether Parliament will in future adopt them. Equity never had anything to do with criminal law, though there are certain cases in which an injunction can be granted to restrain the commission of a crime. But the Star Chamber, which in some ways bore the same relation to the Common Law Courts on the criminal side as the Chancery had to the Common Law Courts on the civil side, created some crimes, such as perjury, libel, and attempts to commit crimes, which were not known to the medieval common law. Piracy, which is practically robbery (even a frustrated attempt at robbery) committed against a ship at sea, and which was at one time punished by the Admiralty Court, has also been taken up in the criminal common law.

2. *Civil and criminal law contrasted*

The difference between civil law (which has formed the main subject of the previous chapters) and criminal law turns on the difference between two different objects which the law seeks to pursue—redress or punishment. The object of civil law is the redress of wrongs by compelling compensation or restitution: the wrongdoer is not punished, he only suffers so much harm as is necessary to make good the wrong he has done. The person who has suffered gets a definite benefit from the law, or at least he avoids a loss. On the other hand, in the case of crimes, the main object of the law is to punish the wrongdoer; to give him and others a strong inducement not to commit the same or similar crimes, to reform him if possible, and perhaps to satisfy the public sense that wrongdoing ought to meet with retribution. But this punishment is not directly or mainly beneficial to the person injured, though a scheme whereby the State pays compensation *ex gratia* to victims of crimes of violence was started in 1964. If a fine is imposed it goes to the State; if the criminal is imprisoned the injured man or his relations may feel some satisfaction, but the satisfaction of their feelings ought not to be regarded as the object of the punishment, though efforts to ensure that punishment should appear to be just to the victim, the public, and the offender are shown by some of the detailed provisions of the Criminal Justice Act 1991.

An interesting attempt to deter crime is found in the Criminal Justice Act 1972, which confers on courts the power to confiscate property used for the purpose of crime, and this power has been increased by the Criminal Justice Act 1988. Under this power there have been several cases where courts have confiscated the motor cars of those convicted of siphoning petrol out of other people's cars in a period of petrol shortage. Analogous powers created in an effort to deter the drug trade are contained in the Drug Trafficking Offences Act 1986. In all cases of crime the law treats the wrongdoing as not merely an injury to an individual, but as a matter of public concern. An individual suffering civil injury need not sue the wrongdoer, and may contract not to sue him. Where a crime has been committed, the person injured cannot prevent proceedings being taken to secure punishment, and an agreement not to prosecute is a criminal offence. Criminal proceedings are taken in the name of the Queen as representing the State, every citizen has a right to set the law in motion whether he has been injured or not, and public officers exist to set the law in motion where necessary. The Queen can pardon the vast majority of crimes after and even before conviction; but the Queen cannot pardon a civil wrong done to a private person, so as to deprive him of his remedy. So, again, the Queen can, through the Attorney-General, stop a criminal prosecution, but she cannot stop a civil action.

Many crimes may be committed without giving anyone a right to bring a civil action: e.g. treason, and forgery where no one has been defrauded, so too perjury. On the other hand, many or most civil wrongs are not crimes: e.g. trespass where no wilful damage is done is no crime, and the notice that 'trespassers will be prosecuted' has been well described as 'a wooden falsehood'. In some cases, however, the same act is both a crime and a civil wrong, as in the case of injuries to the person and defamatory libel, and in general it may be said that any criminal act which causes damage to an individual is civilly actionable. In such cases both civil and criminal proceedings may, with some exceptions, be taken for the same act: it is not necessary to choose between the two, but the proceedings are quite distinct. Only in some exceptional cases can punishment and redress be obtained in the same proceedings. Thus, in the case of a conviction for theft, the court may order the restitution of the goods to the owner; and a court may, upon convicting an accused person of any offence, order the payment of compensation by the accused for any personal injury, loss, or damage to property caused by his offence. A judicial separation may be obtained in proceedings by a wife against her husband on the ground of aggravated assault.

3. *Classification of crimes and offences*

Criminal offences may be broadly divided into two main classes: indictable offences, and offences punishable on summary conviction before magistrates. In the case of indictable offences (which in general comprise the more serious offences) the process of indictment used to be preceded by an inquiry before a magistrate or magistrates, who decided whether there was sufficient evidence to send the case for trial, but this preliminary process has been abolished by the Criminal Justice and Public Order Act 1994. The trial takes place before a judge or recorder at the Crown Court, with a jury in all cases except where the accused pleads guilty; the jury, subject to the right of the accused to appeal, finally decides whether he is guilty or not. If they bring in a verdict, either that he is guilty or that he is not guilty, he can never be tried again for the same offence.

Magistrates, who sit without a jury, have also a considerable statutory power, most recently increased by the Criminal Justice and Public Order Act 1994, of dealing summarily with indictable offences. In the case of a child, that is to say one who has reached the age of 10 but is not yet 14 years, or a young person, that is one who has reached 14 but is not yet 17, they have virtually exclusive jurisdiction in any crime except homicide, unless the child or young person is charged jointly with a person over 16. The summary jurisdiction over adults is more restricted; it does not cover the graver offences. Its exercise is also subject to the consent of the prosecution in cases concerning the property or affairs of the sovereign or certain public bodies. In all cases of indictable crime tried by magistrates, there are special limits to the amount of punishment which they can impose. Accused persons who can prove that they are too poor to afford the cost of legal defence can obtain free legal aid.

Indictable offences are classified in a way which corresponds generally with the seriousness of the offence. At the head we have the offence of treason, which stands in a class by itself. Other indictable offences used to be divided into felonies and misde-meanours. At a time when felonies, with one exception, were punishable with death, and in any case involved forfeiture of the felon's property, the distinction was one of great importance; but by the mid-twentieth century it was an anachronism, and it was abolished by the Criminal Law Act 1967. The distinction is now replaced by one between those offences for which a person may be arrested and those for which he may not. Arrestable offences are all those for which the sentence is fixed by law (such as murder, for which there is a mandatory sentence of life imprisonment), or for which a person may, on first conviction, be sentenced to imprisonment for a term of at least five years, and all attempts to commit such offences.

In the case of offences punishable summarily the magistrate or magistrates decide the whole case without a jury, and impose the punishment. This class of case includes certain indictable offences if the accused consents to be tried summarily (but no consent is necessary in the case of a 'child' or 'young person'); and in these cases the magistrates may impose a sentence of not more than six months' imprisonment, or a fine, or both. It also includes a great number of minor offences: petty assaults, petty forms of dishonesty, cruelty to animals, failure to send one's children to school, riding a bicycle at night without a light and, most important of all, motoring offences which do not cause death. Where a person accused of any one of these minor offences (except assault) is liable to imprisonment for more than three months, he has a right, if he chooses to insist on it, to be tried by indictment, i.e. to have trial by jury.

4. *General principles*

The Criminal Law consists for the most part of the definition (often elaborate and even verbose, especially when Statute Law has intervened) of the conduct which is necessary to constitute a crime; and the number of species and varieties of crime is so large that no detailed account is here possible, nor would a bare enumeration serve any useful purpose. It is, however, generally the rule that an act will not in itself be criminal, unless it is done intentionally, recklessly, with guilty knowledge, or maliciously. But in some exceptional cases the accused may be convicted even though his action was neither intentional, nor reckless, nor even negligent. This is often the case where statutes have been designed simply to prevent certain conduct from occurring, such as the parking of a car in a restricted area.

There are some immoral and dishonest acts which, whether for good reasons or bad, incur no punishment; but in general the prohibitions of the criminal law correspond with the moral sense of the community, and with few exceptions crimes are acts from which every man knows he ought to refrain. It will be enough to say something of the general principles of liability, and to deal with a few points of interest in connection with particular crimes.

In general the law punishes only acts and not omissions. The cases where an omission to perform a legal duty amounts to a crime arise chiefly in connection with homicide, and will be dealt with under that head, or with negligence in driving motor vehicles. Further, an involuntary act, such as that done by a person walking in his sleep, involves no criminal liability. Involuntary intoxication, as for example where a person's drink has been tampered with, may sometimes negate intention to commit a crime, but lack of control caused by knowingly consuming alcohol or drugs will not do so. An act done under compulsion or under stress of necessity is still a voluntary act, and it is only in extreme cases that necessity or compulsion can be pleaded as a defence to a criminal charge. It was held that shipwrecked sailors who killed a boy in order to preserve their lives by eating his body were guilty of murder. Coercion by threats of instant death or grievous bodily harm may, however, excuse participation in a crime less than murder. It is hardly necessary to say that the fact that an act is done from a sense of moral or religious duty is no defence.

Ignorance that an act is criminal is no excuse. In some cases, however, the definition of a crime requires that the offender should know that he is violating some private right, and here ignorance even of a general rule of law may be material. Thus the taking of another's goods is no offence (though it is a civil wrong) if it is done in assertion of a supposed right. Ignorance of fact, on the other hand, is to a very large extent a complete defence. A person who acts in the honest and reasonable belief that facts exist which would make his act entirely innocent incurs no liability in the case of all the more serious crimes. A woman who married, honestly and on reasonable grounds believing that her first husband who had left her was dead, was held not guilty of bigamy, although he had not been absent for seven years, in which case she would have been expressly protected by statute. On the other hand, where a crime is so defined by statute that some circumstance is an essential part of it, the question may arise whether the intention was to punish the act whenever accompanied by the circumstance specified, or only when done with knowledge of the circumstance. To pass false money unwittingly is, by statute, no offence; to sell adulterated food is an offence, though one believes it to be unadulterated. In some cases it seems to be material that the act, even if done in the circumstances supposed by the prisoner to exist, would have been criminal or illegal, and perhaps even that it would have been immoral.

The word 'maliciously', which often occurs in the definition of crimes against property, means no more than that the act must be done intentionally and without justification or excuse or claim of right. Malice in connection with criminal libel has the same meaning as in the law of torts. The meaning of 'malice afore-thought' in relation to homicide will be discussed later.

Those who actually commit offences and those who aid, counsel, or procure their commission are all equally punishable. Under the Criminal Law Act 1967 there are also penalties for concealing arrestable offences, for giving false information to the police, and for assisting offenders.

The law punishes not only crimes actually committed, but also steps towards the commission of a crime which may never be completed. Such steps are incitements, attempts, and conspiracies. It is impossible to define precisely how closely an act must be connected with an intended crime to constitute an attempt, though the law on attempts has now been codified by the Criminal Attempts Act 1981. In practice little difficulty seems to arise. Procuring dies for the purpose of coining false money is an attempt to commit that crime; buying a firearm in order to commit a murder would not by itself be an attempt to murder. The 1981 Act provides that a person is guilty of attempting to commit an offence if with intent to commit that offence he does an act which is more than merely preparatory to the commission of the offence. An act may be an attempt, though the commission of the crime was from the beginning impossible, e.g. there may be an attempt to steal from an empty pocket. But the

House of Lords held in 1985 that there cannot be a conviction for a criminal attempt if, whatever the accused's belief, on the true facts he could never have committed an offence had he gone beyond his attempt so as to achieve fruition, e.g. where he believed he was handling stolen goods, but they were not in fact stolen.

The common law crime of conspiracy has been partly replaced by the effect of the Criminal Law Act 1977, which provides for a statutory offence of conspiracy where two or more persons agree to commit a crime. This is punishable by a fine or, where the crime intended would have been punishable by imprisonment, by imprisonment not exceeding the maximum penalty for that crime. But the Act expressly preserves two other types of conspiracy under the old common law: (*a*) conspiracy to defraud, and (*b*) conspiracy to corrupt public morals or outrage public decency. In a case of 1962 the House of Lords held that there had been a criminal conspiracy to corrupt public morals where persons had agreed to publish a 'Ladies Directory', giving the names, addresses, and practices of prostitutes. The 1977 Act, however, provides that it is no longer an offence to incite or attempt the crime of conspiracy; and agreements, in contemplation or furtherance of a trade dispute, to commit summary offences which are not punishable with imprisonment are excluded from the offence of conspiracy.

5. *High treason*

Of the forms of high treason defined in the Treason Act 1351 only three are now of practical importance: 'Compassing or imagining the King's death', 'levying war against the King in his realm', and 'adhering to the King's enemies in his realm, giving them aid and comfort in the realm or elsewhere'. These words have been overlaid by a mass of judicial interpretation, the effect of which has been to convert treason from being mainly a breach of personal allegiance into a crime against the security of the State. With regard to the first of these forms of high treason, the 'imagining', which seems at first sight a mere matter of intention, must, as is shown by the words of the statute itself, be proved by 'open deed', which includes writing and printing, but not mere spoken words, unless they are spoken in furtherance of the intention which they express. It is settled that to constitute imagining the Queen's death it is sufficient if there is an intention to depose, or even an intention to levy war against the Queen, or to incite foreigners to invade the Queen's dominions.

'Levying war' again has been extended by judicial interpretation so as to include insurrections against the Government, and even insurrections for any general public object (e.g. in the eighteenth century it was held treason to cause an insurrection for the purpose of destroying all dissenting meeting-houses). The Emergency Powers Act 1920 gives the Government very extensive powers, in cases where the action of bodies of persons threatens to deprive the community of the essentials of life, to make regulations giving powers to officials and others to secure these essentials.

The offence can only be committed by a British citizen, or by a non-citizen who is for the time being under the Queen's protection, which he is taken to enjoy if he is resident in British territory or, if not resident, he has left 'family and effects' therein, or continues to possess a valid British passport, of whose potential benefits he has made no overt renunciation. A British citizen cannot obtain immunity to fight against his country by becoming naturalized in a hostile state when war has broken out or is on the point of breaking out.

In the thirty years before 1914 only one prosecution for treason took place in England. The prisoner was convicted, but the death sentence (still the penalty for treason) was commuted, and he was released later. In the war of 1914–18 one prisoner was convicted in the High Court and executed; another succeeded in an appeal against his conviction. The war of 1939–45, however, produced a larger crop of treason cases. In peacetime, offences connected with espionage for foreign powers and the passing of secret information to foreign agents etc. are provided for by a series of Official Secrets Acts. In 1977 the Law Commission suggested that treason should no longer be a crime in peacetime, but that new offences should be created to deal with rebellion, and to protect the personal security of the Monarch and Monarch's immediate family. Legislation along these lines has not yet, however, been enacted.

6. *Incitement to disaffection*

By an Act passed in 1934 it is an offence punishable by a maximum of two years' imprisonment or a fine, or both imprisonment and fine, to attempt maliciously and advisedly to seduce any member of Her Majesty's forces from his duty or allegiance. A person having in his possession documents with intent to commit or aid this offence is also guilty of an offence, provided that the dissemination of these documents to Her Majesty's forces would amount to the commission of the offence of seducing them from their duty or allegiance. A judge of the High Court may, if satisfied by information on oath that there is reasonable ground for thinking that this offence has been committed, direct the issue of a search warrant to discover documents or other evidence of its commission; but in practice little use has been made of this offence.

7. *Public order offences*

The Common Law rules designed to maintain order at assemblies in public places had become strained by the higher incidence of violence occurring in the 1980s and 1990s, occasioned sometimes by political motivation and more often by partisan groups at or in the vicinity of sporting events, especially football. Much of the old law has now been replaced, therefore, by the Public Order Act 1986 (reinforced by the Football (Offences) Act 1991) which specifies new, more clearly defined, offences. Thus the offence of violent disorder, punishable by five years' imprisonment, is committed where three or more persons present together use or threaten unlawful violence, and their conduct is such as would cause a person of reasonable firmness present at the scene to fear for his personal safety. Riot, punishable by ten years' imprisonment, is committed in the same way by twelve or more persons, provided they have a common purpose. An affray is of a similar nature to violent disorder, but may be committed by a person acting alone. Other new offences created by the 1986 Act include causing harassment, alarm, or distress.

If the police reasonably apprehend that a meeting, though initiated by persons themselves peaceful, is likely to cause disturbance which must be taken to have been anticipated by those persons, they may, and indeed must, request those persons to hold the meeting elsewhere, and the persons, if they refuse to move, may be convicted of resisting the police in the execution of their duty. It has also been decided that the police have a right to enter and remain on any premises in order to prevent the commission of any offences whatever, including the utterance of seditious speeches, if they have a reasonable apprehension that such acts are likely to be committed.

The Public Order Act 1936 originally gave the police powers to impose on those organizing a public procession conditions necessary for preserving public order, and to prescribe the route to be taken by it. These powers are now increased by the Public Order Act 1986, and written notice must be given of public processions intended to demonstrate support of, or opposition to, any person or body of persons, or to mark or commemorate any event, unless it is not reasonably practicable to give advance notice. The organizers commit an offence if they fail to satisfy these requirements, or if in general the conduct of the procession differs from that indicated in the notice. Police may impose conditions upon, or request a ban of, a public procession.

The 1936 Act also prohibits the wearing of uniforms signifying membership of a political organization in a public place or at a public meeting, and the training of the members of such organizations in such a way that they are able to usurp the functions of the police or the army. Section 5 of that Act made it an offence for any person, in any public place or at any public meeting, to use threatening, abusive, or insulting words or behaviour, with intent to provoke a breach of the peace or whereby a breach of the peace is likely to be occasioned, but the 1986 Act redefines this offence by reviewing the requirement of intent to provoke or of occasioning a breach of the peace, thus making it more likely that convictions for intimidation will be secured.

A related statute is the Race Relations Act 1976, replacing two earlier statutes of the same name, and complementing the Sex Discrimination Act 1975, which has been mentioned earlier in this book (p. 60). Under this legislation discrimination is prohibited, with only a few exceptions, against any person on grounds of his sex, colour, race, nationality, or ethnic or national origins. Many of the provisions of the 1976 Act are so designed as to give a right of redress either in the civil courts or in specialist tribunals, but there is also a special conciliation procedure designed to avert the necessity for such proceedings in most cases. However there were also certain provisions creating criminal offences, and these have been strengthened by the Public Order Act 1986 and the Criminal Justice and Public Order Act 1994. It is now an offence to use words, display written material, or behave in such a way as to threaten, abuse or insult anyone by reason of colour, race, nationality, or ethnic or national origins, if it is intended that racial hatred be stirred up, or if racial hatred is likely to be stirred up thereby. Publication or distribution to the public of written material of this character is also an offence; and possession of racially inflammatory material is an offence.

8. *Libel, sedition, and obscenity*

A seditious libel is one calculated to bring into hatred or contempt, or to excite disaffection against, the Queen, the Government and Constitution, either House of Parliament, or the administration of justice; to excite the Queen's subjects to attempt otherwise than by lawful means the alteration of any matter in Church or State by law established; to raise discontent or disaffection, or to promote feelings of ill-will or hostility between different classes.

The definition is a wide one, but the fact that the decision whether anything published is or is not a seditious libel rests with the jury prevents a Government from using the law for punishing expressions of opinion which meet with any considerable degree of popular approval. And it is clear that an honest criticism or statement of errors committed by the Government, or of evils in the constitution, with a view to their reform or removal by lawful means is not seditious. The speaking of seditious words is equally punishable with the publication of a seditious libel.

Blasphemous libel is committed by any person publishing in a permanent form an attack on Christian doctrine, God, Christ, the Bible, or the formularies of the Church of England, provided that it is calculated to outrage and insult the feelings of believers. The accused must have intended to publish the material, though not necessarily to outrage and insult Christian believers. Spoken words which are blasphemous are equally punishable. It may be that the concept of criminal blasphemy is outdated now, and the Law Commission has suggested its abolition and replacement by a new offence of using threatening, insulting or abusive words or behaviour in a place of worship. This would have the merit, in what has become a multiracial society with many differing religious beliefs, of extending the protection of religious susceptibilities beyond those of the Church of England or of Christianity, but limiting the operation of criminal law in this area to the control of acts or behaviour inside places of worship. To date, however, no legislation along these lines has been forthcoming.

For purposes of criminal law, defamatory libels include not only libels which would be actionable as torts, but also libels on the character of deceased persons, if intended to wound the feelings of the living. Further, a libel is sufficiently published to be criminally punishable if communicated merely to the person whose character is attacked. The proof of the truth of a defamatory libel affords no defence to a criminal prosecution unless it is also shown that the publication was for the public benefit. The defences of privilege and of fair comment are as available in a criminal prosecution as in a civil action. In 1985 the Law

Commission recommended the replacement of Common Law criminal libel by a more restricted offence limited to cases of deliberate character assassination, but this has not yet been adopted.

All forms of libel are punishable by fine and imprisonment, though prosecutions are rare. But the speaking of words which would only be actionable civilly as slander is not a criminal offence.

Any person who publishes, whether for gain or not, an obscene article is, by the Obscene Publications Act 1959, guilty of an offence punishable summarily with six months' imprisonment or a fine of £100, or both, or, on indictment, with imprisonment for three years or a fine, or both. An 'article' is anything which contains or embodies matter to be read or looked at, or it may be a cinematograph exhibition, a film or a sound record, or anything used for the manufacture or reproduction of obscene articles, such as photographic negatives, stencils, and moulds. The Theatres Act 1968 makes it a similar offence (punishable summarily with six months' imprisonment or a fine of £400, or, on indictment, with imprisonment for up to three years or a fine, or both) to present or direct, whether or not for gain, an obscene performance of a play in public or in private. An article or play is deemed to be obscene if its effect, or the effect of any of its items, is, taken as a whole, such as to tend to deprave and corrupt (either sexually or in any other way, such as by inducing drug addiction) persons who are likely, having regard to all relevant circumstances, to read, see, or hear the matter contained in it. There is provision also for the seizing of obscene articles, and the Obscene Publications Act 1964 adds the offence of possession of any obscene article for publication for gain, even though publication has not yet taken place. The Indecent Displays (Control) Act 1981 makes it an offence to display publicly or to cause or permit the public display of indecent matter, though exceptions to this provision include television broadcasts, plays, cinematograph exhibitions, art galleries and museums. The main purpose of the 1981 Act was to prohibit the open display on bookstalls of magazines with nude or sexually explicit photographs on their covers.

Defences include excusable ignorance and innocent dissemination, or that publication is for the public good. The latter defence lets in proofs of literary or artistic merit, and it enabled Penguin Books Ltd. to obtain an acquittal when prosecuted under the 1959 Act for publishing D. H. Lawrence's book, *Lady Chatterley's Lover*.

9. *Homicide*

Punishable homicide falls into three categories, (*a*) murder, (*b*) manslaughter, (*c*) causing death by dangerous driving of a motor vehicle.

The taking of life is unlawful and amounts to murder whenever it is done by an act which is to cause death or grievous (that is, really serious) bodily harm, unless the act can be justified on special grounds, such as the prevention of crime and the arrest of offenders, or the right of self-defence, the limits of which are somewhat narrowly defined. (The termination of pregnancies by medical practitioners is lawful in circumstances specified by the Abortion Act 1967.) In 1985 the House of Lords held that the necessary intent for murder does not, as the courts had previously found, exist where the accused only knew that death or grievous bodily harm was likely to result from his act (as where he had shot his stepfather when they had both been playing a game with shot-guns while drunk); he must have actually foreseen that consequence as a natural result of what he was doing. But where a victim died from blows delivered by three attackers it was held that all three must have foreseen his death as a likely consequence, so that whichever of them delivered the fatal blow was guilty of murder. This particular criminal intent, which must be proved before a jury may convict the accused of murder, is called 'malice aforethought'.

There is, however, no general duty to preserve life.

> Thou shalt not kill, but needst not strive
> Officiously to keep alive

is generally true in our law. A man who, seeing another

struggling in the water, stands by and lets him drown, when he might have saved him by throwing a rope, is guilty of no crime. It would only be when a man is guilty of a high degree of culpable negligence in failing to carry out a legal duty tending to the preservation of life that he would be guilty of the other main unlawful homicide, manslaughter, if death ensues in consequence of his omission. Such negligence is known as 'criminal negligence'. The duty may be one imposed by contract (as in the case of a railway signalman); or by a special relation between the parties (as in the case of a parent's duty to provide for children too young to provide for themselves, or where a couple had taken in a sick relative as a lodger, and had failed to feed her or obtain any medical help for her); or by statute. Thus the Maritime Conventions Act 1911 imposes on a person in charge of a ship the duty of rendering assistance to anyone in danger of being lost at sea, if assistance can be given without serious danger; and regulations made under the Road Traffic Acts impose various duties as to the user of motor vehicles. There may also be a legal duty to take precautions in doing an act which is dangerous if precautions are omitted (e.g. the duty of a motorist to keep his brakes effective).

It is still the rule, except possibly in the case of category (*c*), that an act which causes death is not homicide if the death occurs more than a year and a day after the commission of the act, but the Law Commission has now recommended abolition of the rule, especially because modern medical technology enables victims of violence to be kept alive on life-support machines for very long periods.

It was only in 1956 that the legislature in any way took charge of the field of homicide. In that year, owing to the notorious reluctance of juries to convict of 'motor manslaughter', the specific offence of causing death by reckless or dangerous driving was created, and it is now provided for as causing death by *dangerous* driving by the Road Traffic Act 1991. It is punishable with imprisonment for five years.

Manslaughter, it has been said, 'may extend from the verge of murder to the verge of excusable homicide'. Thus intentionally to push a paving stone off a railway bridge on to an oncoming train, killing the guard who was sitting next to the driver, was held in 1976 to be manslaughter, as the act was unlawful and dangerous, but only inadvertently caused death; and there was a similar decision in the case of men who threw a concrete block from a bridge on to a motorway, killing a taxi driver who was taking a miner to work during the miners' strike of 1984–5. The maximum punishment is imprisonment for life, the minimum a short term of imprisonment, a mere fine, or even discharge (absolute or conditional). The crime has been made even more elastic by the Homicide Act 1957, which reduces to manslaughter certain acts which would previously have been treated as murder:

(*a*) Where a person can prove that, in being a party to the killing of another, he was under such mental abnormality, caused by injury, disease, or arrested development, as substantially impaired his mental responsibility. This may cover a killing under 'irresistible impulse' (see p. 67).

(*b*) Where the jury decide that the killer was provoked to such a degree that a reasonable man would have acted as he did.

(*c*) Where two persons have agreed to commit suicide together, and the pact is carried out by the one party, not having been revoked by the other. If the survivor fails to kill himself, while not *actively* assisting the other party to the pact to kill himself, he is guilty instead of complicity in that other's suicide, under the Suicide Act 1961.

Apart from these special cases, the dividing line is still that the essential ingredient in murder is malice aforethought. An unlawful act or omission which causes death amounts to murder if it is promoted by an intention to kill or cause grievous bodily harm (whether to the person killed or to another). A killing no longer, as in the past, amounts to murder merely because it occurs in the process of (i) resisting lawful arrest, or (ii) the commission of some other violent offence, such as assault or rape, i.e. sexual intercourse obtained by force or deception. But if the accused causes death in circumstances amounting to criminal negligence, or else as a result of doing an unlawful act 'such as all sober and reasonable people would inevitably recognize must subject the other person to, at least, the risk of some harm resulting therefrom, albeit not serious harm' (as Lord Justice Edmund Davies put it in 1966), he will be guilty of manslaughter.

During the last two and a half centuries the courts have progressively narrowed substantially their acceptance of acts as amounting to involuntary manslaughter. In the eighteenth century manslaughter was held to be committed if death was caused in the course of committing *any* unlawful act. But now the act must be criminally unlawful, dangerous, directed at the victim, and likely to cause immediate injury, however slight. Thus it has been held in recent years that manslaughter has not been committed merely by supplying a dangerous drug to someone who then died as a result of taking an overdose. Nevertheless the rules established by the courts have been found difficult to apply in practice, especially in cases involving surgeons or anaesthetists who make small, but fatal, errors in the course of an operation, and also in cases where deaths result from the actions of corporations, such as the disaster caused by the capsizing of a car ferry just outside the port of Zeebrugge. The Law Commission is now actively considering the whole area of involuntary manslaughter, and is expected to issue its report on the subject before long.

By the Murder (Abolition of Death Penalty) Act 1965, the punishment for murder is a mandatory life sentence, and the court convicting may recommend a minimum period of imprisonment before any possible release on licence. In no case may the Home Secretary release a murderer on licence without first consulting the Lord Chief Justice and, if possible, the trial judge.

The Infanticide Act 1938 provides that if a woman causes the death of her newly born child, and it appears that the balance of her mind was disturbed as the result of the birth, she is to be punished only as if guilty of manslaughter.

10. *Offences against property*

The law relating to offences against property was in earlier times an extraordinary tangle made up of Common Law rules overlaid by piecemeal legislation. But this was replaced by the Theft Act 1968 (together with certain later amendments) and the Criminal Damage Act 1971, which virtually provide a new code of law over most of the range of crimes concerning property.

The core of this branch of the law is the crime of theft (stealing). It involves, as its essential elements, a dishonest appropriation of property belonging to another with the intention of permanently depriving the other of it. The offence will be committed even if there is no intention to benefit from the theft. 'Appropriation' involves an assumption of the rights of an owner, and it may include the keeping of property which a person has come by innocently, unless he purchased it in good faith. Thus, if Charles takes a book out of John's brief-case as a practical joke, but then decides later to keep it, he will be guilty of theft. The 1968 Act, however, provides that the accused will have a defence to a charge of theft if the appropriation was made with a claim of right, however mistaken, or in the belief that the owner would have consented, or that the owner could not reasonably be discovered. The Criminal Attempts Act 1981 creates the offence of interference with a motor vehicle or trailer, an interesting modern example of an offence resulting from an act which falls short of theft.

Land cannot normally be stolen. But a trustee or other person with authority to sell or dispose of land who appropriates the land by dealing with it in breach of the confidence reposed in him will be guilty of theft. So will anyone who appropriates anything forming part of the soil, or growing out of it (such as crops), or built upon it, by severing it from the rest of the land. Wild animals do not count as 'property', unless they are in a state of captivity, or have been 'reduced into possession' by being killed, and thus only in these latter circumstances may they be stolen. The poaching of game, and killing or taking of deer or fish, are, however, still punishable under certain nineteenth-century statutes, and under the Criminal Justice and Public Order Act 1994 an aggravated trespass is committed by anyone going on to private land with the intention of disrupting a lawful activity. This new offence is intended to counter the increasingly violent behaviour of those seeking to disrupt or sabotage hunting. By the Criminal Law Act 1977 it is a summary offence for any person, without lawful authority, to use or threaten violence for the purpose of securing entry to any premises, provided that there is someone on the premises opposed to the entry and this is known to the person trying to enter. But it is a defence for the accused to prove that he was, or was acting on behalf of, a displaced residential occupier. Thus no offence is committed by a person who, on returning home from work, finds that his house has been occupied by squatters and uses force to get inside.

Theft is punishable with a maximum of ten years' imprisonment; but aggravated forms of it—e.g. robbery (that is, stealing with the use of force or a threat of force) and assault with intent to rob—are punishable with life imprisonment. Burglary, punishable with fourteen years' imprisonment, is committed by entering a building as a trespasser with intent to commit theft, rape, grievous bodily harm, or criminal damage; or else by committing like offences after having entered as a trespasser. But burglary committed by any person having with him a firearm or offensive weapon is punishable with life imprisonment. Obtaining property or a pecuniary advantage by a deception carries a maximum penalty of ten years' imprisonment, but blackmail, which is committed by making an unwarranted demand with menaces, is punishable with fourteen years' imprisonment. Dishonestly handling stolen goods, knowing or believing them to be stolen, is also punishable with fourteen years' imprisonment, because the existence of dishonest handlers is often the spur needed for thieves to go about their stealing. On a deterrent basis, if it were possible to stamp out handling it would seem that much stealing would cease.

Frauds and misappropriations by agents, trustees, directors and officers of companies and corporations are offences. The law of forgery has been codified by the Forgery and Counterfeiting Act 1981. The offence consists in the making of a false instrument in order that it may be used as genuine. 'Instruments' covers a wide variety of documents, e.g. money orders, share certificates, passports, stamps, discs, tapes and information recorded or stored by mechanical or electronic means; and the Act makes separate provision for the offence of counterfeiting currency notes and coins. Intentional or reckless destruction of or damage to another's property is punishable, under the Criminal Damage Act 1971, with ten years' imprisonment, or, if done by fire, with life imprisonment. In this latter case of fire the offence is still known by the old name of arson.

Breach of contract is very rarely punishable. It is, however, a crime for workmen to break their contracts of service where the probable consequence will be to endanger life or valuable property, or to deprive a place of its supply of gas or water; and if a person is employed by a local or other public authority it is a crime to break such a contract, if the probable consequence will be to cause injury or danger or grave inconvenience to the community.

Notes

Chapter 2

1. Some of the most burdensome of these incidents were *Wardship and Marriage*—the lord had the right to the wardship of the lands of his deceased tenant's infant heir and was not accountable for the profits, and when the heir came of age he could marry him or her to anyone he chose; if the heir refused to marry the person proposed he had to pay the value of the marriage, i.e. the sum which the person proposed as wife or husband was willing to pay the lord for the marriage; *Reliefs*—a sum due from a tenant when he succeeded to his father's estate; *Escheat*—the right which the lord had to take back the land if the tenant died without heirs or, until 1870, if he committed a felony. All these liabilities could be got rid of by a conveyance to uses—a fact which goes far to account for their popularity.

Chapter 5

1. The most important of the Property Acts were as follows: the parts of the Law of Property Act 1922 which were unrepealed; the Law of Property Act 1925; the Land Charges Act 1925; the Settled Land Act 1925; the Trustee Act 1925; the Administration of Estates Act 1925; the Land Registration Act 1925. Some of these Acts have since been amended or replaced, notably by the Law of Property Act 1969, the Land Charges Act 1972, the Land Registration Acts 1966, 1986, and 1988, the Land Registration and Land Charges Act 1971, and the Law of Property (Miscellaneous Provisions) Acts 1989 and 1994.
2. The unfree tenure was that of villeins. When in the sixteenth century these became personally free, the peculiarities of their tenure remained under the name of copyhold, which was abolished in 1922, and all its incidents extinguished by 1936.
3. In two cases real property stands outside the trust for sale, which attaches, as we have seen to the property of an intestate:

   1. Where the owner of an entailed interest in possession dies without taking advantage of the power to devise it which is, as we have seen, conferred on him by the legislation of 1925.

2. Where a mentally disordered person, of full age at the end of 1925, and unable, because of his condition, to make a will, dies possessed of real property, without having recovered his testamentary capacity. This case will disappear before long by effluxion of time.

In these two cases, the real property descends according to the rules laid down in the statutes of 1833 and 1859.

Recourse must also be had to these rules in yet a third case which has nothing directly to do with intestacy. If any kind of property is given by an instrument, whether testamentary or *inter vivos*, expressly to the heir of a deceased person, the settlor or testator has used a technical expression belonging to the old law, and the legislation of 1925 logically provides that the heir must be sought by reference to that old law.

4. The unmodified provisions of the Act of 1925, under which property devolved between 1 January 1926 and 31 December 1952, may be summarized as follows:

A surviving spouse took the personal chattels, and £1,000 free of death duties. If there was issue, the survivor took a life interest in half the remaining estate, the other half, and the future interest in the half taken by the survivor, being held by the intestate's representative on the statutory trusts for the issue. If there was no issue, the survivor took a life interest in the whole of the remaining estate; but was entitled to the remaining estate absolutely only in the event of there being no relations within the degrees enumerated on pp. 126–8.

Further reading

Legal theory

The student of law faces a vast storehouse of literature on the subject, but it is possible to pick out a small selection of works which are the most useful for those embarking upon legal study. The classic account of English legal theory is provided by Sir Carleton Allen, *Law in the Making* (Clarendon Press), which is written in a particularly attractive style, but is nevertheless a bit dated. Modern texts include M. D. A. Freeman (ed.), *Lloyd's Introduction to Jurisprudence* (Sweet & Maxwell), which gives a good account of the different schools of jurisprudence; R. W. M. Dias, *Jurisprudence* (Butterworth); and G. W. Paton, *A Textbook of Jurisprudence* (Clarendon Press). A very popular account of a modern viewpoint by a leading jurist is H. L. A. Hart, *The Concept of Law* (Clarendon Press). Collections of specialist essays may be found in A. G. Guest (ed.), *Oxford Essays in Jurisprudence* (Clarendon Press); A. W. B. Simpson (ed.), *Oxford Essays in Jurisprudence (second series)* (Clarendon Press); and J. Eekelaar and J. Bell (eds.), *Oxford Essays in Jurisprudence (third series)* (Clarendon Press). A clear and accurate account of the working of the doctrine of precedent will be found in Sir Rupert Cross, *Precedent in English Law* (Clarendon Press). The relationship of law to the needs of society is explored in P. S. Atiyah, *Law and Modern Society* (Oxford University Press).

Law and its history

A comprehensive account of English law as a whole in the eighteenth century is contained in the four volumes of Sir William Blackstone, *Commentaries* (Sweet & Maxwell). But an overall coverage of English law at the present day is best seen in O. Hood Phillips and A. H. Hudson, *A First Book of English Law* (Sweet & Maxwell); or P. S. James, *Introduction to English Law* (Butterworth). Both books are particularly designed for beginners. The best modern account of English legal history is probably provided by S. F. C. Milsom, *Historical Foundations of the Common Law* (Butterworth), though J. H. Baker, *Introduction to English Legal History* (Butterworth) is also useful. Other works on legal history which may be consulted include T. F. T. Plucknett, *A Concise History of the Common Law* (Butterworth); H. Potter, *Historical Introduction to English Law* (Sweet & Maxwell); and H. Potter, *Outlines of English Legal History* (Sweet & Maxwell). The most complete coverage of English legal history is in the sixteen volumes of Sir William Holdsworth, *A History of English Law* (Methuen), but two shorter collections of Holdsworth's papers on specialist topics are especially worthy of perusal: *Some Makers of English Law* (Cambridge University Press), and *Sources and Literature of English Law* (Clarendon Press).

Equity and trusts

The three leading works at present are probably P. H. Pettit, *Equity and the Law of Trusts* (Butterworth); H. G. Hanbury and R. H. Maudsley, *Modern Equity* (Stevens); and A. J. Oakley, *Parker and Mellows: The Modern Law of Trusts* (Sweet & Maxwell). A classic volume of lectures delivered the best part of a century ago, but still providing stimulation for thought and understanding, is F. W. Maitland, *Lectures on Equity* (Cambridge University Press). L. A. Sheridan and G. W. Keeton, *The Law of Trusts* (Barry Rose), and G. W. Keeton and L. A. Sheridan, *Equity* (Pitman) may be consulted, and useful collections of cases and materials may be found in R. H. Maudsley and E. H. Burn, *Trusts and Trustees: Cases and Materials* (Butterworth); and J. A. Nathan and O. R. Marshall, *A Casebook on Trusts* (Stevens).

Family law

The main textbooks on the law of persons are P. M. Bromley, *Family Law* (Butterworth); and S. M. Cretney, *Family Law* (Sweet & Maxwell). Other works include J. Dewar, *Law and the Family* (Butterworth); H. B. Grant and J. Levin, *Family Law* (Sweet & Maxwell); B. M. Hoggett, *Parents and Children* (Sweet & Maxwell); B. Passingham, *Law and Practice in Matrimonial Causes* (Butterworth); and O. M. Stone, *Family Law* (Macmillan). A shorter book which may be found particularly helpful by beginners is S. M. Cretney, *Elements of Family Law* (Sweet & Maxwell).

Property law

The best account of the law of property as it was before the great reforms of 1925 is in A. W. B. Simpson, *An Introduction to the History of the Land Law* (Clarendon Press); but an admirable short account of the law which provides a bridge to the modern system is A. D.

Hargreaves, *Introduction to the Principles of Land Law* (Sweet & Maxwell). The modern law is stated comprehensively in Sir Robert Megarry and H. W. R. Wade, *The Law of Real Property* (Stevens); and G. C. Cheshire and E. H. Burn, *Modern Real Property* (Butterworth); but a shorter account may be found in Sir Robert Megarry, *A Manual of the Law of Real Property* (Stevens). F. H. Lawson and B. Rudden, *The Law of Property* (Clarendon Press), is probably best studied after reading the larger works, because it is a mature reflection upon the whole nature of this area of the law. Other general works are J. G. Riddall, *Introduction to Land Law* (Butterworth); and the collection of source materials in R. H. Maudsley and E. H. Burn, *Land Law: Cases and Materials* (Butterworth). On specialist areas of property law, books worthy of consultation include S. J. Bailey, *Law of Wills* (Pitman); Sir Desmond Heap, *An Outline of Planning Law* (Sweet & Maxwell); A. E. Telling, *Planning Law and Procedure* (Butterworth); J. C. Vaines, *Personal Property* (Butterworth); and J. Phillips, *Introduction to Intellectual Property Law* (Butterworth).

Law of contract

The law of contract is well served by three major textbooks: Sir William Anson, *Principles of the English Law of Contract* (Clarendon Press); G. C. Cheshire, C. H. S. Fifoot, and M. P. Furmston, *The Law of Contract* (Butterworth); and G. H. Treitel, *The Law of Contract* (Stevens). Two introductory works, G. H. Treitel, *An Outline of the Law of Contract* (Butterworth), and P. S. Atiyah, *An Introduction to the Law of Contract* (Clarendon Press), are helpful, but both will stretch the beginner. A somewhat more concise book is J. C. Smith, *The Law of Contract* (Sweet & Maxwell). A valuable sourcebook containing much explanatory material is J. C. Smith and J. A. C. Thomas, *A Casebook on Contract* (Sweet & Maxwell); and a companion volume to the authors' textbook is G. C. Cheshire, C. H. S. Fifoot, and M. P. Furmston, *Cases on the Law of Contract* (Butterworth). An advanced conceptual exposition is provided by P. S. Atiyah, *The Rise and Fall of Freedom of Contract* (Oxford University Press); and a useful account of the law of both contract and torts is P. J. Cooke and D. W. Oughton, *The Common Law of Obligations* (Butterworth).

Law of torts

The law of torts is equally well provided with major textbooks: Sir John Salmond and R. F. V. Heuston, *The Law of Torts* (Sweet & Maxwell);

H. Street, *The Law of Torts* (Butterworth); and Sir Percy Winfield and J. A. Jolowicz, *Tort* (Sweet & Maxwell). Introductory books are J. G. Fleming, *An Introduction to the Law of Torts* (Clarendon Press); W. V. H. Rogers, *The Law of Tort* (Sweet & Maxwell); and P. S. James and D. J. L. Brown, *General Principles of the Law of Torts* (Butterworth); while a useful specialist work is G. L. Williams and B. A. Hepple, *Foundations of the Law of Tort* (Butterworth). C. D. Baker, *Tort* (Sweet & Maxwell) is a concise book covering the whole subject without aspiring to great depth. Sources are well presented in B. A. Hepple and M. H. Matthews, *Tort: Cases and Materials* (Butterworth); and J. A. Weir, *A Casebook on Tort* (Sweet & Maxwell).

Criminal law

The most satisfactory short textbook on criminal law is Sir Rupert Cross, P. A. Jones, and R. Card, *Introduction to Criminal Law* (Butterworth), to which there is a companion work, *Cases on Criminal Law* (Butterworth). But the leading major textbook is J. C. Smith and B. Hogan, *Criminal Law* (Butterworth). A possible alternative textbook is A. Ashworth, *Principles of Criminal Law* (Clarendon Press); and a short, clear, and directly stated work is M. J. Allen, *Textbook on Criminal Law* (Blackstone Press). The main rival textbook today is G. L. Williams, *Textbook of Criminal Law* (Stevens). J. C. Smith, *The Law of Theft* (Butterworth) is an accurate and comprehensive account of a prime area of criminal law. Sir James Stephen, *Digest of the Criminal Law* (Macmillan), though dating from the nineteenth century, is worthy of some attention as it is a statement of the law in the form of a code, which has again become relevant in the last quarter of the twentieth century because of the wave of codification of many parts of the criminal law.

The courts

The most comprehensive account of the organization and procedure of the courts is to be found in R. J. Walker and M. G. Walker, *The English Legal System* (Butterworth). K. J. Eddey, *The English Legal System* (Sweet & Maxwell) is a short account of the same subject; while there is a good coverage, written from a contemporary rather than historical angle, in P. J. Smith and S. H. Bailey, *The Modern English Legal System* (Sweet & Maxwell).

Constitutional and administrative law

What lawyers now generally call public law is served by a wide variety of publications. The major textbooks on constitutional law are S. A. de Smith, *Constitutional and Administrative Law* (Penguin); O. Hood Phillips, *Constitutional and Administrative Law* (Sweet & Maxwell); and E. C. S. Wade and A. W. Bradley, *Constitutional and Administrative Law* (Longman), each devoting a portion of their space to the application of constitutional principles in the form of administrative law. Sir David Yardley, *Introduction to Constitutional and Administrative Law* (Butterworth), provides a much shorter account, which is specially designed for beginners. Sir Ivor Jennings, *The Law and the Constitution* (University of London Press), is now rather dated, but still provides some stimulus for thought, as does the even older A. V. Dicey, *The Law of the Constitution* (Macmillan), which contains the famous lectures delivered by the Vinerian Professor in Oxford over a century ago. A companion volume to Professor Hood Phillips's textbook is O. Hood Phillips, *Leading Cases in Constitutional and Administrative Law* (Sweet & Maxwell); and an alternative is D. Polland and D. Hughes, *Constitutional and Administrative Law—Text and Materials* (Butterworth).

The major textbooks on administrative law proper are Sir William Wade, *Administrative Law* (Clarendon Press); P. Craig, *Administrative Law* (Sweet & Maxwell); and J. F. Garner, *Administrative Law* (Butterworth); and a useful sourcebook is S. H. Bailey, B. L. Jones and A. Mowbray, *Cases and Materials in Administrative Law* (Sweet & Maxwell). D. L. Foulkes, *Administrative Law* (Butterworth) has grown in size with successive editions, but is still a fair guide for beginners in the subject. J. F. McEldowney, *Public Law* (Sweet & Maxwell) provides some different slants on the subject.

Index